Ontologies in the Behavioral Sciences

Accelerating Research and the Spread of Knowledge

Committee on Accelerating Behavioral Science
through Ontology Development and Use

Robert M. Kaplan and Alexandra S. Beatty, *Editors*

Board on Behavioral, Cognitive, and Sensory Sciences

Division on Behavioral and Social Sciences and Education

A Consensus Study Report of

The National Academies of
SCIENCES • ENGINEERING • MEDICINE

THE NATIONAL ACADEMIES PRESS
Washington, DC
www.nap.edu

THE NATIONAL ACADEMIES PRESS   500 Fifth Street, NW   Washington, DC 20001

This activity was supported by contracts between the National Academy of Sciences and the American Psychological Association, Association for Psychological Science, Federation of Associations in Behavioral & Brain Sciences, National Cancer Institute, National Institute on Aging, National Library of Medicine, National Science Foundation (1729167), and National Institutes of Health Office of Behavioral and Social Sciences Research (OBSSR) (HHSN263201800029I/75N98020F00010). Any opinions, findings, conclusions, or recommendations expressed in this publication do not necessarily reflect the views of any organization or agency that provided support for the project.

International Standard Book Number-13: 978-0-309-27731-0
International Standard Book Number-10: 0-309-27731-0
Digital Object Identifier: https://doi.org/10.17226/26464

Additional copies of this publication are available from the National Academies Press, 500 Fifth Street, NW, Keck 360, Washington, DC 20001; (800) 624-6242 or (202) 334-3313; http://www.nap.edu.

Copyright 2022 by the National Academy of Sciences. All rights reserved.

Printed in the United States of America

Suggested citation: National Academies of Sciences, Engineering, and Medicine. 2022. *Ontologies in the Behavioral Sciences: Accelerating Research and the Spread of Knowledge.* Washington, DC: The National Academies Press. https://doi.org/10.17226/26464.

The National Academies of
SCIENCES · ENGINEERING · MEDICINE

The **National Academy of Sciences** was established in 1863 by an Act of Congress, signed by President Lincoln, as a private, nongovernmental institution to advise the nation on issues related to science and technology. Members are elected by their peers for outstanding contributions to research. Dr. Marcia McNutt is president.

The **National Academy of Engineering** was established in 1964 under the charter of the National Academy of Sciences to bring the practices of engineering to advising the nation. Members are elected by their peers for extraordinary contributions to engineering. Dr. John L. Anderson is president.

The **National Academy of Medicine** (formerly the Institute of Medicine) was established in 1970 under the charter of the National Academy of Sciences to advise the nation on medical and health issues. Members are elected by their peers for distinguished contributions to medicine and health. Dr. Victor J. Dzau is president.

The three Academies work together as the **National Academies of Sciences, Engineering, and Medicine** to provide independent, objective analysis and advice to the nation and conduct other activities to solve complex problems and inform public policy decisions. The National Academies also encourage education and research, recognize outstanding contributions to knowledge, and increase public understanding in matters of science, engineering, and medicine.

Learn more about the National Academies of Sciences, Engineering, and Medicine at **www.nationalacademies.org**.

The National Academies of
SCIENCES · ENGINEERING · MEDICINE

Consensus Study Reports published by the National Academies of Sciences, Engineering, and Medicine document the evidence-based consensus on the study's statement of task by an authoring committee of experts. Reports typically include findings, conclusions, and recommendations based on information gathered by the committee and the committee's deliberations. Each report has been subjected to a rigorous and independent peer-review process and it represents the position of the National Academies on the statement of task.

Proceedings published by the National Academies of Sciences, Engineering, and Medicine chronicle the presentations and discussions at a workshop, symposium, or other event convened by the National Academies. The statements and opinions contained in proceedings are those of the participants and are not endorsed by other participants, the planning committee, or the National Academies.

For information about other products and activities of the National Academies, please visit www.nationalacademies.org/about/whatwedo.

COMMITTEE ON ACCELERATING BEHAVIORAL SCIENCE THROUGH ONTOLOGY DEVELOPMENT AND USE

ROBERT M. KAPLAN[1] (*Chair*), Department of Medicine, Primary Care, and Population Health, Stanford University
DEMBA BA, Brain Science Initiative, Harvard University
LISA FELDMAN BARRETT, College of Science, Northeastern University
JIANG BIAN, Department of Health Outcomes and Biomedical Informatics, College of Medicine, University of Florida
KATY BÖRNER, Luddy School of Informatics, Computing, and Engineering, Indiana University
BRUCE F. CHORPITA, Department of Psychology, University of California, Los Angeles
DAVID DANKS, Halıcıoğlu Data Science Institute and Department of Philosophy, University of California, San Diego
KARINA W. DAVIDSON, Feinstein Institutes for Medical Research, Northwell Health
RANDALL W. ENGLE,[2,3] School of Psychology, Georgia Institute of Technology
CATHERINE A. HARTLEY, Department of Psychology and Center for Neural Science. New York University
MARK A. MUSEN,[1] Center for Biomedical Informatics Research, Stanford University
VIMLA L. PATEL, Center for Cognitive Studies in Medicine and Public Health, New York Academy of Medicine
FRANK PUGA, School of Nursing, University of Alabama at Birmingham
CARLA SHARP, Department of Psychology, University of Houston
TIMOTHY J. STRAUMAN, Institute for Brain Sciences, Duke University
CUI TAO, School of Biomedical Informatics, University of Texas Health Center at Houston
JAMES F. WOODWARD, Department of History and Philosophy of Science, University of Pittsburgh

ALEXANDRA S. BEATTY, *Study Director, Senior Program Officer*
TINA M. WINTERS, *Associate Program Officer*
J. ASHTON BULLOCK, *Senior Program Assistant*

---

[1] Member, National Academy of Medicine.
[2] Member, National Academy of Science.
[3] Resigned from committee May 2021.

BOARD ON BEHAVIORAL, COGNITIVE, AND SENSORY SCIENCES

TERRIE E. MOFFITT[1] (*Chair*), Duke University
RICHARD N. ASLIN,[2] Yale University
JOHN BAUGH, Washington University in St. Louis
WILSON S. GEISLER,[2] University of Texas at Austin
MICHELE GELFAND,[2] University of Maryland, College Park
ULRICH MAYR, University of Oregon
KATHERINE L. MILKMAN, University of Pennsylvania
ELIZABETH A. PHELPS, Harvard University
DAVID E. POEPPEL, New York University
STACEY SINCLAIR, Princeton University
TIMOTHY J. STRAUMAN, Duke University

SAMANTHA CHAO, *Acting Director*

---

[1] Member, National Academy of Medicine.
[2] Member, National Academy of Sciences.

Preface

There are few people whose lives have not been touched in some way by behavioral science research. Topics of study in this domain range from developmental and abnormal psychology to political science, sociology, and behavioral economics. Findings from this work guide diagnosis and treatments of mental disorders, shape policy, and help people make sense of individual behavior and individuals' relationship to the world around them. These disciplines are flourishing in many ways, but progress—as in any science discipline—requires that scientists share a common vocabulary. Over the last few decades, incentives to innovate in the behavioral sciences have resulted in a proliferation of theories, constructs, and measures, which has led to a range of problems in both building and applying knowledge. The link between these challenges for the behavioral sciences and the comparative lack of development of ontologies in these fields has attracted increasing attention. Ontologies—systems for assigning definitions to the concepts that are important in a particular domain—sound arcane but are in fact fundamental to scientific progress. Other scientific domains have made greater progress in establishing unified languages and shared conceptualizations, and this project's sponsors, among others, recognized that improved ontologies will be critical to accelerating progress in the behavioral sciences. We thank the project's sponsors: at the National Institutes of Health, the Office of Behavioral and Social Sciences Research, the National Institute on Aging, the National Library of Medicine, and the National Cancer Institute; the National Science Foundation; the American Psychological Association; the Association for Psychological Science; and the Federation of Associations in Behavioral and Brain Sciences. They collaborated in developing the statement of task for the study and also provided valuable perspectives to the committee as we began our work.

The committee also gratefully acknowledges the support and contributions of many individuals. They include the scholars who participated in our two public workshops, providing us with valuable information about example ontologies and perspectives on challenges and opportunities to advance them (in the order in which they presented to the committee): David Danks, University of California, San Diego (who later joined the committee); Russell Poldrack, Stanford University; Deborah McGuinness, Rensselaer Polytechnic Institute; Thomas Insel, Stanford University; Bruce Cuthbert, the National Institute of Mental Health; Benjamin Lahey, University of Chicago; Susan Michie, University College, London; Robert West, University College, London; Sandro Galea, Boston University School of Public Health; Howard Koh, Harvard T.H. Chan School of Public Health; Kathryn Phillips, University of California San Francisco; and Richard Moser and Lyubov Remennik, National Cancer Institute.

The committee also gratefully acknowledges the time that Anne Harrington, Harvard University, and Kenneth Kendler, Virginia Commonwealth University, spent answering our questions. We also thank Randall Engle, Georgia Institute of Technology, who had to resign from the committee very early in the project.

The committee commissioned five scholars to look more deeply at a number of questions. We thank the authors for producing excellent resources for the committee in record time: David Cella, Northwestern University, and Ronald Hays, University of California Los Angeles; Christopher Chute, Johns Hopkins University; Louise Falzon, the University of Sheffield; Janna Hastings, University College, London; and Kenneth Kendler, Virginia Commonwealth University.

I also want to express special gratitude to my fellow committee members who took time away from their busy schedules to delve into this complicated problem. This report is about shared conceptualizations and common scientific languages, and the committee itself was composed of experts from a wide range of academic backgrounds. Despite the fact that the project coincided with the COVID-19 pandemic and therefore had to be conducted almost entirely by Zoom, our work was characterized by a high degree of mutual respect and collegiality. Each member made significant contributions and each of us came away with a deeper appreciation for cross-disciplinary communication.

Finally, we owe very special thanks to Alexandra (Alix) Beatty, our exceptionally talented and experienced study director. Not only did Alix manage every decision and scrutinize every word in this report, she also ensured that the project remained on time. On multiple occasions the committee argued that it was not possible to produce the report on the scheduled timeline: Alix, with great poise and empathy, politely but firmly explained that taking more time was not an option. We were ultimately pleased that she kept us on track while insisting on the highest level of quality. We also owe gratitude to Tina Winters for overseeing the technical aspects of constructing the report and many other challenging tasks and to Ashton Bullock for overseeing the administrative and logistical details.

This Consensus Study Report was reviewed in draft form by individuals chosen for their diverse perspectives and technical expertise. The purpose of this independent review is to provide candid and critical comments that will assist the National Academies of Sciences, Engineering, and Medicine in making each published report as sound as possible and to ensure that it meets the institutional standards for quality, objectivity, evidence, and responsiveness to the study charge. The review comments and draft manuscript remain confidential to protect the integrity of the deliberative process.

We thank the following individuals for their review of this report: Michael Anderson, Brain and Mind Institute, University of Western Ontario; John Graybeal, Stanford University; Gizem Korkmaz, Biocomplexity Institute & Initiative, University of Virginia; Benjamin Lahey, Biological Sciences Division, The University of Chicago; Russell Poldrack, Department of Psychology, Stanford University; Jodi Schneider, School of Information Sciences, University of Illinois Urbana-Champaign; William Stead, Vanderbilt University; Frank van Harmelen, Computer Science Department, Vrije Universiteit Amsterdam; Timothy Wilson, Department of Psychology, University of Virginia.

Although the reviewers listed above provided many constructive comments and suggestions, they were not asked to endorse the conclusions or recommendations of this report nor did they see the final draft before its release. The review of this report was overseen by Cynthia M. Beall, Department of Anthropology, Case Western University, and Bernice A. Pescosolido, Department of Sociology, Indiana University. They were responsible for making certain that an independent examination of this report was carried out in accordance with the standards of the National Academies and that all review comments were carefully considered. Responsibility for the final content rests entirely with the authoring committee and the National Academies.

Coming together to produce this report has been an exceptional experience. When we began the process, many of us did not understand the depth of problems caused by mismatched conceptualizations, information overload, and lost opportunities to develop more coherent behavioral sciences. We leave the process with a better understanding of the issues and the promise that integrating the behavioral sciences with information and computer sciences will lead to the acceleration of knowledge.

> Robert M. Kaplan
> *Chair*, Committee on Accelerating
> Behavioral Science through Ontology
> Development and Use

Contents

SUMMARY   1

1 INTRODUCTION   9
  Context, 11
    A Long History of "Classification", 11
    Particular Challenges in the Behavioral Sciences, 15
  Committee's Approach to Its Charge, 16
    The Behavioral Sciences, 16
    Use Cases, 18
  Study Process: Four Key Questions, 21
  Guide to This Report, 23
  References, 24

2 WHY ONTOLOGIES MATTER   27
  Challenges with Synthesizing and Applying Knowledge, 30
  Challenges with Generalizing Research Findings, 34
  Challenges with Building and Structuring Knowledge, 35
    Challenges with Classification, 36
    Challenges with Defining Constructs, 38
    Challenges with Measuring Constructs, 39
  Summary, 42
  References, 43

3 UNDERSTANDING ONTOLOGIES — 49
Defining *Ontology*, 49
A Continuum of Semantic Specification, 52
Examples of Ontological Systems, 56
    A Formally Specified Ontology: The Behavioral Change Intervention Ontology, 56
    Classification Systems for Mental Health Problems, 60
    A Categorical Classification System: The Diagnostic and Statistical Manual of Mental Disorders, 60
    A Dimensional Classification System: Research Domain Criteria, 63
    A Quantitative Approach: The Hierarchical Taxonomy of Psychopathology, 66
Conclusions, 67
References, 68

4 HOW ONTOLOGIES FACILITATE SCIENCE — 73
How Ontologies Facilitate Scientific Progress, 74
    Clarifying the Phenomena That Are Studied, 74
    Classification, 75
    Communication, 77
    Data Integration, 79
    Data Sharing, 80
    Bibliographic Retrieval, 81
    Comparison and Analysis of Data, 82
Primary Benefits of Ontologies, 83
    Improving Patient Care, 84
    Building Infrastructure for Scientific Research, 84
    Expanding Scientific Knowledge, 85
Conclusion, 86
References, 86

5 ENGINEERING BEHAVIORAL ONTOLOGIES — 89
Existing Behavioral Ontologies, 89
The Ontology Engineering Process: Socio-Cognitive Practices, 98
    Creation, 98
    Change and Evolution, 100
    The Role of Institutions, 101
    Evaluation, 103

The Ontology Engineering Process: Computational Tools, 104
   Creation and Editing, 105
   Dissemination, 108
   Evaluation and Debugging, 109
   Potential Directions for the Future, 110
Needed Institutional and Organizational Support, 112
   Discovery, 112
   Capacity, 113
   Practices, 113
Conclusions, 114
References, 115

6 **CONCLUSIONS AND RECOMMENDATIONS**   121
   The Need for Ontologies in the Behavioral Sciences, 121
   Strengthening Ontology Use in the Behavioral Sciences, 124
   Supporting and Sustaining Behavioral Ontologies, 126
   References, 132

APPENDIXES

A	Ontological Systems Referenced in the Report	133
B	Example Use Cases Generated in a Committee Self-Survey	135
C	Biographical Sketches of Committee on Accelerating Behavioral Science through Ontology Development and Use	143

Summary

Collectively, humans now know more about behavior than at any point in history. The pace of scientific discovery is unprecedented, with new clinical trials and experimental research being published every day. Yet despite these advances, the behavioral sciences—the social and biological sciences concerned with the study of behavior—face substantial challenges. Inconsistent use of terms and classification systems makes it challenging to integrate findings from individual studies and in turn to cumulatively build bodies of knowledge even in domains that are consistently studied. Furthermore, knowledge generated by behavioral science research is not efficiently translated for the consumers who will apply it to benefit individuals and society. The gap between what is known and the capacity to act on that knowledge has never been larger, and it continues to grow.

Ontologies provide a way to address these and other challenges in the behavioral sciences. Scientists use the word *ontology* to refer to efforts to structure and manage the ways in which they formally describe the entities in their discipline. Ontologies build on the philosophical notion of classifying ideas, particularly those related to the nature of existence. A widely accepted definition of a scientific ontology is a formal, explicit specification of a shared conceptualization: a commitment to using a precise, agreed-upon set of terms and relationships to represent a domain. This clear semantic specification is key to addressing the behavioral sciences' challenges and accelerating scientific progress.

The National Academies of Sciences, Engineering, and Medicine formed a committee to study ways to improve the development and use of ontologies in the behavioral domain with support from four divisions of the National

Institutes of Health (the Office of Behavioral and Social Sciences Research, the National Institute on Aging, the National Library of Medicine, and the National Cancer Institute), the National Science Foundation, the American Psychological Association, the Association for Psychological Science, and the Federation of Associations in Behavioral and Brain Sciences. The committee appointed to conduct the study—which included experts in medicine, population health, psychology, psychiatry, biobehavioral sciences, biomedical informatics, neural and cognitive science, library and information science, the history and philosophy of science, computer science, and bioengineering—was directed to review the relevant literature, as well as example ontologies, to identify advantages and obstacles to the further development of behavioral ontologies, to identify recommended approaches to strengthening ontologies, and to offer conclusions and recommendations for advancing behavioral ontologies.

The committee focused its attention on one segment of the very broad terrain of the behavioral sciences, the domain of mental health, in order to look deeply at the literature, example ontologies, and issues in context. We explored four basic questions:

- Why do ontologies matter?
- What exactly are ontologies?
- How do ontologies facilitate advancement in the behavioral sciences?
- How can the engineering of ontologies in the behavioral sciences be strengthened?

THE BENEFITS OF ONTOLOGIES

A wide variety of stakeholders rely on the knowledge created by the behavioral sciences. Just in the domain of mental health, stakeholders include scientists and clinicians who provide educational, behavioral, social, and psychological interventions, as well as educators, health care practitioners, policy makers, and patients. The quality of the care provided to the millions of people who experience mental disorders depends both on the availability of relevant research and on the capacity of clinicians to distill relevant information from the massive volume of research published every year. The scientists who produce the research seek to test and reproduce their findings and integrate them with other knowledge. The resulting knowledge must be synthesized, generalized, and disseminated so it can be applied. Without formal ontologies, all of these functions are more difficult than they need to be.

The absence of formal ontologies—shared understanding of the concepts and phenomena being studied—also undermines the research itself. Scientists' work is shaped by their understanding of the concepts and entities they are studying and how they are categorized, decisions about ways to measure the phenomena of interest accurately, and decisions about what is and is not germane to their research investigations. Progress in the behavioral sciences has been hindered by the use of different terms or descriptions for the same underlying entity or condition; the use of the same term for different entities or concepts; the use of different, poorly correlated measures for the same entity; and the use of measures whose relationship to the phenomena they are measuring is not well understood. A lack of ontological clarity makes it difficult to synthesize, replicate, and generalize research findings. A key consequence is that it is difficult to build on existing knowledge, which then leads to challenges for retrieving and acting on research.

By establishing shared terms for the concepts and phenomena of interest within a particular domain and a classification of those entities, ontologies make key scientific functions possible. A clear and explicit ontology allows scientists to be precise about what they are studying and how they think about the domain in which they are working, and about the relationships among concepts, including how they are classified. By articulating a shared conceptualization of the phenomena of interest, an ontology allows scientists to communicate about ideas among themselves and with the rest of the world.

Shared ontologies help researchers to integrate their data with data developed by others, or to perform secondary analysis of online datasets. Shared ontologies make it possible for computer systems to exchange scientific claims about theories and data, thereby allowing for the development of intelligent systems and survey instruments that acquire and process data in standardized ways. Perhaps most important, ontologies make scientific research much more readily accessible not only to scientists but also to consumers, including patients searching for information relevant to their health and to practitioners who offer health services. In addition to offering scientists the direct benefits of formal specifications of entities and relationships, ontologies support scientific work indirectly, providing a foundation for scientists' efforts to develop cumulative knowledge bases, make predictions, and develop causal explanations.

STRENGTHENING EXISTING ONTOLOGIES IN THE BEHAVIORAL SCIENCES

The committee identified numerous valuable efforts to bring ontological clarity to behavioral science but found comparatively few well-developed behavioral ontologies. A number of ontological systems that enumerate essential entities in the discipline have been developed for specific purposes and do not necessarily meet the definition of *ontology*. Many existing efforts have been isolated, and it appears that their adoption has been constrained. Moreover, the developers of behavioral ontologies appear to operate primarily on their own in identifying or developing the models and practices that might best suit their particular needs.

To better understand the path forward for the behavioral sciences, the committee examined the two basic components of the process of engineering formal and clear ontologies: the socio-cognitive practices and the computational tools that support the process. The socio-cognitive practices involved in creating and editing an ontology and adapting it over time require intensive human involvement. Computer tools can bring extremely valuable efficiency to the development, maintenance, and editing of ontologies, but they can never stand in for the human understanding, ingenuity, and social perceptions that go into the development and use of ontologies.

Taking advantage of opportunities to strengthen ontologies in the behavioral sciences will require attention to the practical challenges of supporting the work required. There are only a few examples of ontology development efforts in the behavioral sciences that have endured. The primary—perhaps the most important—reason for this situation is that the development and the maintenance of ontologies are both time consuming and expensive. There is no substitute, in pursuing such an effort, for the human time and intellectual effort needed, not only for the initial effort but also on an ongoing basis, as ontologies need be to continually evaluated and updated. Despite the many efficiencies afforded by computer technology, developing an ontology for any area of science is painstaking. Particularly within the behavioral sciences, there has been a lack of sustainable resources.

On the basis of these findings, the committee reached 10 conclusions:

1. Classification systems in the behavioral sciences that serve valuable ontological purposes lie on a continuum of semantic specification.
2. The classification systems that currently are widely used in the behavioral sciences do not have formal semantics, and therefore they do not readily provide opportunities to support automated reasoning and other artificial intelligence applications.
3. Ontological systems with the most formal semantic specification are not necessarily superior to others, but they offer the greatest opportunities for accelerating the behavioral sciences through the use of artificial intelligence. The most important characteristic of an ontological systems is that the level of formal specificity fits the intended purpose of the ontological system.
4. By establishing a controlled vocabulary of shared terms for the concepts and phenomena of interest within a particular domain and a classification of those entities, ontological systems have three primary benefits: opportunities to improve outcomes (care and services), infrastructure to support the mechanics and application of contemporary scientific research, and enhanced capacity to expand scientific knowledge.

5. Valuable ontological systems and related tools exist and are supporting research in the behavioral sciences. However, many of these efforts have been isolated, resources to support them (including training and education) have been limited, and the developers of ontological systems are mainly on their own to identify or develop the models, tools, and approaches that might best advance research and practice.
6. Ontology engineering rests on two foundations: socio-cognitive functions and the use of computational tools that support the process.
7. To provide the intended benefits, an ontology should be logically sound, valid, and usable by a diverse range of stakeholders.
8. For ontology engineering to progress in the behavioral sciences, sustained resources and specific actions and processes are needed for discovery, capacity building, and the promotion of practices and processes.
9. Ontology development and use has the potential to move behavioral science forward from a domain in which research is generally siloed and the data and results are often incompatible to one in which the evidence is searchable and more easily integrated and in which computer technology is leveraged.
10. Because there is no existing funding mechanism for the development and maintenance of ontological systems and the tools that support them in the behavioral sciences, sustained public and private support for the long-term development, dissemination, and maintenance of ontologies and related tools are needed.

RECOMMENDATIONS

The committee recognizes that developing and using ontologies may require complicated tradeoffs. It is possible that too much emphasis on ontological rigor could hinder originality or discourage the unorthodox thinking that has led to major scientific advances. Yet, although existing ontological systems have served valuable purposes, taken together they have not exploited the large potential for ontologies to accelerate advancement and application of behavioral research. It may be that some domains of the behavioral sciences have more to gain from a focus on ontology development than others. The committee expects that increased use of ontologies in the behavioral sciences is likely to involve different and sometimes parallel ontologies. Especially in the near term, "ontologic pluralism," in which competing or overlapping ontologies exist but are connected to one another through formal mapping, is both inevitable and desirable.

The committee does not believe that ontologies can be expected to develop organically without encouragement: that approach has yielded the current situation. Therefore, we focused on ways to expand available resources and incentives, stimulate grassroots ontology development, and coordinate efforts, with the aim of pushing for ontologies to be a higher priority in behavioral science research. An infrastructure is needed to coordinate and support this effort. Agencies of the federal government are the entities best positioned to provide the coordination and resources needed for this work, so we direct three of our recommendations to the National Institutes of Health, the National Science Foundations, and other federal agencies. We direct the other three to professional organizations.

RECOMMENDATION 1: The National Institutes of Health (NIH) and the National Science Foundation (NSF) should develop formal agendas for accelerating behavioral science research through the development and use of semantically formal ontologies. These agendas should draw on ideas generated within other scientific domains and the international scientific community and should include a range of activities:

- NIH should use its convening authority to engage experts and to develop a plan for ontology development across NIH institutes and centers. The plan should illustrate how NIH resources might be used to develop ontologies; link them to existing ontologies; and apply them in the interest of higher quality, more replicable behavioral research, and improved behavioral health, including through criteria for funding research efforts.
- Within NIH, the Behavioral and Social Science Coordinating Committee should propose a plan for ontology development across NIH institutes and centers.
- The NIH Division of Program Coordination, Planning, and Strategic Initiatives should develop an ontology for classifying intramural and extramural behavioral research at NIH.
- The NSF Social, Behavioral and Economic Science Directorate should coordinate ontology development efforts with the NSF Computer, Information Science, and Engineering Directorate.
- NIH and NSF should collaborate in providing transition grants to allow ontology centers to develop business plans and distribution models that could put them on a sustainable footing.
- The National Library of Medicine should bolster the training it offers in biomedical informatics to strengthen the capacity of the people who will lead the development of the next generation of scientific ontologies.

- To avoid duplication and overlap, NIH and NSF ontology development efforts should be coordinated through the NIH Office of Behavioral and Social Sciences Research and the NSF Social, Behavioral, and Economic Sciences Directorate.

RECOMMENDATION 2: The National Institutes of Health, the National Science Foundation, and other agencies that support research should seek and encourage opportunities to fund work that will support continuing progress in the development and use of ontologies in the behavioral sciences, such as research on technological supports for ontology development, the ways scientists develop and use ontologies across diverse fields, and institutional supports and structures that support ontology use in diverse fields.

RECOMMENDATION 3: The Office of Science and Technology Policy should develop a report on how an explicit formal specification of a shared conceptualization for behavioral science can be implemented across federal science agencies, based on review of ontologies developed by other agencies, including, but not limited to, the National Science Foundation; the Departments of Health and Human Services, Defense, Transportation, Agriculture, Labor, and Justice; the Environmental Protection Agency; the National Institute of Standards and Technology; the National Oceanic and Atmospheric Administration; and the Defense Advanced Research Projects Agency.

Professional organizations and publishers also have a key role to play, and we direct three recommendations to such organizations. We call out specific organizations in part because they have broad reach, but we hope that similar organizations will also take part in the community building necessary to develop and encourage understanding of what ontologies can offer in the behavioral sciences.

RECOMMENDATION 4: The Federation of Associations in Behavioral and Brain Sciences and the Consortium of Social Science Associations, along with similar organizations, should coordinate ontology development across academic and professional organizations.

RECOMMENDATION 5: The American Psychological Association Council of Editors and the Association for Psychological Science editorial office, along with similar organizations, should develop policies to improve the use of common vocabularies and data reporting standards in behavioral science journals.

RECOMMENDATION 6: The Council of Graduate Departments of Psychology, the Education Directorate of the American Psychological Association, and the Education Office of the Association for Psychological Science, along with similar interested organizations, should create strategies to integrate ontology development into graduate-level teaching and practical training.

The committee's conclusions and recommendations build on what has been accomplished through centuries of attempts to synthesize what is known, as well as decades of research on human behavior. The actions recommended have the potential to make that knowledge more efficiently retrievable and actionable by a wide diversity of stakeholders. The committee hopes to contribute to improvement in the way knowledge is accumulated and synthesized in behavioral science and related fields. Ultimately, better communication within the scientific community and between scientists and knowledge consumers will improve the science of behavior, the way it is disseminated, and its capacity to ameliorate and prevent suffering. This report is focused on the behavioral sciences, but most of the issues discussed here would apply in other domains as well. The committee hopes these insights will be of use in advancing science generally.

1

Introduction

Charles Dickens opened his epic novel *A Tale of Two Cities* with the statement, "It was the best of times, it was the worst of times." In many ways, the behavioral sciences are in the best of times. Collectively, humans now know more about behavior than at any point in our history as a species. The pace of scientific discovery is unprecedented, with new clinical trials and experimental research published every day. Psychology, neuroscience, cognitive science, and other fields that build understanding of experiences and behaviors are among the most popular undergraduate majors. The number of published papers in these fields is growing at an exponential rate. Behavioral scientists are among respected experts serving on advisory panels in medicine, law, education, defense, business, and public policy.

Yet despite these advances, the behavioral sciences are facing substantial challenges that constrain scientific progress. These challenges, which ironically have been exacerbated by the many research possibilities opened up by rapid advances in computer technology, hamper the integration of findings from individual studies to accumulate bodies of knowledge. They complicate the efficient transmission of this knowledge to the consumers who can use it to benefit individuals and society. Although concerns about the "wealth of information" problem have been noted for decades (e.g., Simon, 1971), the gap between what is known and the capacity to act on what is known has never been larger, and it continues to grow. In this respect, the behavioral sciences are in the worst of times.

This report examines how a stronger commitment to the use of ontologies—formal systems for organizing knowledge—can help to address these and related challenges in the behavioral sciences. The National

Academies of Sciences, Engineering, and Medicine formed a committee to study ways of accelerating the behavioral sciences by improving the development and use of ontologies. The work was supported by four divisions of the National Institutes of Health (the Office of Behavioral and Social Sciences Research, the National Institute on Aging, the National Library of Medicine, and the National Cancer Institute), the National Science Foundation, the American Psychological Association, the Association for Psychological Science, and the Federation of Associations in Behavioral and Brain Sciences. The committee, which included experts in medicine, population health, psychology, psychiatry, biobehavioral sciences, biomedical informatics, neural and cognitive science, library and information science, the history and philosophy of science, computer science, and bioengineering, was charged with reviewing the literature on ontologies in the behavioral sciences and example ontologies in other sciences and developing recommended approaches for improving them; the complete charge is shown in Box 1-1.

BOX 1-1
Statement of Task

An ad hoc committee of the National Academies of Sciences, Engineering, and Medicine will gather, review, and discuss the literature on the development of ontologies in scientific disciplines with a focus on developing the same in the behavioral sciences. The committee will:

- Analyze the literature including a) definitions of components and requirements of ontology development and use; b) highlights of existing or emerging ontologies in the behavioral sciences, their respective advantages and disadvantages, and how they are currently used or could be used; c) descriptions of how ontology use and development in the behavioral sciences can accelerate discovery and enhance replicability and reproducibility.
- Synthesize the advantages and obstacles for behavioral ontology development and use, including provision of compelling use cases that illustrate the need. The use cases should be related to NIH's high priority areas which must be applicable to human health, of trans-disease relevance, and linkable to valid behavioral measures.
- Identify recommended approaches to building behavioral ontologies that are both rigorous and practical to maximize utility and uptake, as well as scientific relevance. This includes recommendations about linking behavioral ontologies across behavioral domains/constructs and to existing biomedical ontologies.

BOX 1-1 Continued

- Draw conclusions and provide recommendations for improving behavioral ontology advancement including:
  - Best practices and parameters for ontology development
  - Resource, infrastructure and training needs
  - Governance principles
  - Identification of high priority research areas
  - Recommendations for enhancing uptake and use in behavioral research
  - Recommendations for sustainability of the ontologies

CONTEXT

A Long History of "Classification"

Attempts to synthesize and summarize what is known about the world date back thousands of years. Scholars and nonscholars alike have faced the problem of how to organize knowledge and to integrate new observations with what is already known. One of the most influential methods of organizing knowledge about the world was launched during the 4th century BC by Aristotle, who attempted to find order among chaos in the natural world: see Box 1-2 and Figure 1-1. In AD 77 Pliny the Elder published *Natural History,* an effort to categorize all that was known. To make it easy to retrieve desired information, he provided a detailed table of contents that guided readers to the departments, or categories of knowledge. The *Fihrist* published by Ibn al-Nadim in 938 was a similar effort to compile and categorize knowledge (in this case a listing of available books) by discipline and topic. Also during the 10th century, scholars in China produced a massive compendium of knowledge, the *Taiping Yulan,* which organized knowledge under 5,000 headings across 55 categories (Blair, 2010). More modern examples emerged during the Enlightenment: for example, Denis Diderot proposed the *Encyclopédie,* co-edited with Jean le Rond d'Alembert and originally published between 1751 and 1772, as a means to fundamentally change how humans think and what humans know. This history suggests that the drive to make sense of and communicate about the world is profoundly human.

Philosophers use the term *ontology* (literally, discourse on being) to describe efforts to classify or group ideas, particularly those related to the nature of existence. Scientists today use the word ontology to refer to efforts to organize knowledge in particular domains. Although there is no

> **BOX 1-2**
> **Aristotle's Animal Ontology**
>
> Among the many accomplishments of the Greek philosopher Aristotle was a system for classification of the animal kingdom. Aristotle identified more than 500 species of living animals and classified them along a ranked scale. The scale used observable features to classify them, such as the organism's number of legs, whether they circulated blood, and whether they were more active during the day or at night. Aristotle regarded the most complex animals as the most perfect, placing humans at the top of the scale and invertebrates, such as insects and mollusks, at the bottom: a primary distinction was between animals that gave birth to live offspring and those that laid eggs. Although Aristotle acknowledged exceptions to the strictly linear ranking of species, later scholars amplified his ideas, identifying sponges and other invertebrates as the lowest level of existence, with insects, fish, amphibians, reptiles, birds, and various mammals at an intermediate level.
>
> Aristotle's animal ontology had a profound effect on the thinking of scholars, clerics, and artists who followed him. Accepting this hierarchy, many artists depicted nonhuman animals looking upward toward humans, and most legal systems treated harm to humans differently from harms to other species. The animal kingdom ontology may also have shaped western theology, in which God was regarded as perfect and other beings as progressively less perfect, depending on their dissimilarities to humans: angels were less perfect than God, but more perfect than humans. Apes were less perfect than humans, but more perfect than other primates.
>
> The animal kingdom ontology example is not just a historical curiosity. Components of Aristotle's ontology guided zoological science for millennia and continue to dominate the way organisms are classified. Yet, the hierarchical scale may have interfered with scientific progress by inhibiting new insights about evolution and adaptation. It was not until the mid-20th century that scholars fully rejected the lower animal-higher animal hierarchy, in favor of understanding that natural selection and environmental adaptation make each organism a "higher" animal for the environmental niche it occupies.
>
> SOURCE: Based on Hodos and Campbell (1969).

universal definition of a scientific ontology, a valuable working definition is an explicit, formal specification of a shared conceptualization—a systematic set of shared terms and an explication of their interrelationships (Gruber, 1995). For a simple example, an ontology might define and categorize types of ice cream products, distinguishing among those served in vessels, in cones, and on sticks, as shown in Figure 1-2.

Today, machine-assisted methods offer feasible, affordable, and scalable supports to the process of organizing knowledge. Computer technology has changed scientific research by making possible many new methods for collecting, sorting, and analyzing increasingly large datasets. Across scientific

FIGURE 1-1 14th-century woodcut of the Ladder of Ascent and Descent of the Intellect, based on Aristotle's hierarchy, by Ramon Lull.
NOTE: The illustration shows God (Deus) at the top of the hierarchy, above angels, humans, types of beasts, and ultimately rocks at the lowest level.
SOURCE: https://commons.m.wikimedia.org/wiki/File:Die_Leiter_des_Auf-_und_Abstiegs.jpg?hcb=1

disciplines, the volume of data generated presents tremendous opportunities, but it also amplifies the challenges of structuring, mining, integrating, and reusing information: those challenges demonstrate the need for and applications of ontologies. Using computer technology to develop and maintain ontologies involving potentially vast quantities of data has offered the potential for significant changes in the ways human beings interact with scientific knowledge.

The natural and biomedical sciences have made substantial progress toward the development and application of accepted ontologies. For example, the Gene Ontology, which was developed by a consortium of researchers and is used around the world, has supported advances and new insights in genetics that would not have been possible without a widely shared, aggregate knowledge base (see Appendix A).[1] Classification systems used in other domains, such as the Iconclass project developed by art historians, which classifies types of images for retrieval, demonstrate growing recognition of the potential for using computer technology to

---

[1] See du Plessis et al. (2011) and Gene Ontology Consortium (2019) for descriptions of the gene ontology and examples of how the ontology is typically used.

FIGURE 1-2 Ontology of ice cream products.
SOURCE: Roz Chast, The New Yorker© Condé Nast.

structure large bodies of data.[2] As in other scientific contexts, ontologies used in the behavioral sciences (e.g., to categorize the components of psychological well-being or to classify thought processes) may help scientists in a variety of ways. In this report we examine how they can help scientists to, for example, link results from diverse research, communicate clearly about complex concepts, more rapidly identify significant knowledge gaps, formulate novel questions, test clear hypotheses, establish whether results can be reproduced, and retrieve and apply scientific knowledge for diverse uses.

---

[2] See https://test.iconclass.org/. Iconclass provides phrases to identify search terms included in the database; a new version of it currently being developed links terms to exemplar images.

Particular Challenges in the Behavioral Sciences

While ontologies have been embraced by many sciences, developing, establishing, and sustaining them has been a significant challenge in the behavioral sciences. Describing and measuring behavioral phenomena is inherently complex, and even in many subfields of study there is a lack of well-established, widely shared definitions for key concepts. The lack of precision in terminology makes it difficult to extract and combine data from diverse research contexts and to understand relationships among phenomena.

Consideration of one example, stress, suggests the scope of the challenge. Stress can be understood as a stimulus (a stressor); a psychological process (e.g., an individual's experience of how stressful the stimulus is); a biological mechanism (e.g., cortisol secretion) that causes some outcome (such as a physiological response or a subjective feeling); or the outcome itself (e.g., feeling stressed). Scientists use the term in studying phenomena as diverse as living in poverty, getting divorced, or experiencing chronic illness, and they do not uniformly specify precisely what they mean by stress in describing their research (Crosswell and Lockwood, 2020). Exposure to situations that cause stress—and responses to stress—are measured with such tools as self-report questionnaires, interviews, and other psychological measurements, and by identifying people exposed to obvious stressors, such as natural disasters. Assessments of physiological responses such as heart rate and cortisol levels have become more common as available technology has advanced (Bellido et al., 2018). Responses to stress can be psychological and behavioral. Signs of stress can include phenomena that may be difficult to isolate, such as anger and irritability, sleep disturbance, or feeling overwhelmed, or health consequences, from headaches to increased risk of cancer or cardiovascular disease. Many factors may influence the effects of stress exposure, including the context and time span of the exposure, the severity of the stressor, the life stage at which it occurs, and the degree to which it is controllable. Moreover, there is no reliable, specific relationship between the presence of a stressful stimulus and its correlates (e.g., sleep disturbance does not always occur in response to stress and can occur in response to other conditions).

Not surprisingly, given this complexity, there is a very large literature on aspects of stress. Yet it is difficult to be sure what "stress" means across these diverse studies, and thus to make informed inferences or broad conclusions about stressors and their effects from the body of research that has explored this multifaceted set of phenomena.

Researchers in the behavioral sciences seek to describe observed phenomena, to understand the causes for those phenomena, to use this knowledge to improve psychological and physical health outcomes, and to predict who might be affected in the future. Yet the distinctions between describing and explaining observed phenomena are not always clear. Even defining the boundaries of the behavioral sciences is challenging. Growing evidence from the study of development, for example, has shown how biological and social influences interact even prenatally to shape gene expression as well as physical and cognitive development (NASEM, 2019). This reality points to the critical importance of research that integrates work from across and beyond the behavioral sciences.

Despite a number of efforts, including the U.K.'s Human Behaviour-Change Project and the Cognitive Atlas (Michie et al., 2017; Poldrack et al., 2011), there are few widely used ontologies in the behavioral sciences; see Chapter 5. The committee was asked to explore reasons to believe that advances in the development of ontologies can help to address the challenges behavioral science researchers face and thereby accelerate progress in these fields. Such progress would not just be of academic interest; it would also hasten the development of interventions that promote health and relieve suffering and support practitioners and others who rely on behavioral research.

COMMITTEE'S APPROACH TO ITS CHARGE

The committee's approach to the charge began with an effort to reach a shared understanding of the meaning of the key terms we were to address, *ontologies* in the *behavioral sciences*, and the basic purposes they serve. Though the committee adopted the most widely used definition of ontology (a formal, explicit specification of a shared conceptualization; Gruber, 1995; see Chapter 3), we acknowledge that both *ontology* and the *behavioral sciences* are terms that lack precise boundaries. Ontology is not a word used frequently in everyday discourse, perhaps even among scientists. Some people may remember the concept from a college philosophy class but have only a hazy recollection of what it really means. A crisp definition of the behavioral sciences may be similarly elusive, but it was important for the committee to identify parameters to guide our work. Chapter 3 discusses the meaning of ontology in more detail;[3] here we review ways to define the behavioral sciences and the general purposes ontologies serve in this context.

The Behavioral Sciences

The development of specific branches of science is a dynamic and evolving process. Indeed, the identification of branches of science across centuries reflects ongoing ontological thinking about categories of knowledge. This shifting landscape makes it hard to derive a consensus definition of any

---

[3] In this report, we generally use the term "ontology" to refer to a range of systems that have been developed to enumerate the essential entities in a discipline, though not all of the systems may meet the precise definition; see Chapter 3 for a detailed discussion.

branch of science, including the behavioral sciences. The Encyclopedia Britannica defines *behavioral science* as any discipline that deals with human behavior or actions (Editors of Encyclopaedia Britannica, n.d.), a definition that would include such disciplines such as psychology, anthropology, sociology, economics, law, psychiatry, political science and the behavioral aspects of biology; the American Psychological Association defines behavioral science as including research on nonhuman animals (Wolman, 1989).

Although the behavioral and social sciences are sometimes regarded as synonymous, some important distinctions can be drawn. The behavioral sciences tend to focus on the study of what happens within and between individuals; the social sciences tend to focus on factors within and across social systems and levels—ranging from those closest to the individual to broad societal and cultural ones—that help to explain complex social behavior. Behavioral scientists may consider system-level influences on behavior, but they are primarily interested in the operationalization and generation of behavioral variables (Adhikari, 2016). The distinction is not crisp, however, because researchers in such fields as social psychology, anthropology, and sociology may blend interest in individuals and groups, taking a more behavioral or a more social approach depending on the target of their investigations. Both classical and behavioral economics are concerned with individual decision making, while political scientists are interested in a host of factors that influence voting and other behavior. Researchers across these domains may use experimental methods (manipulating an independent variable to isolate biological, psychological, or social factors that influence behavior), observational methods and modeling, or they may conduct studies designed to describe or classify behaviors. The behavioral sciences are inherently interdisciplinary, and newer fields of study, such as behavioral economics, continue to challenge traditional disciplinary distinctions.

It is also worth noting the contrasts between the social sciences and the natural sciences and the fact that the behavioral sciences have elements of both. The natural sciences can be said to focus primarily on events in the physical world, that is, phenomena that occur and exist regardless of whether humans perceive them; the social sciences can be said to focus on events in the social world, which is constructed by humans. The behavioral sciences, which focus on the individual or individuals as they are relating to one another, have a foot in both the social and natural camps because they encompass study of the relationships among psychological constructs and underlying biological influences on behavior. Within universities, psychology departments are typically housed in colleges of science, but they are sometimes in colleges of social sciences.

Acknowledging the interdisciplinary nature of the behavioral sciences, we adopt a broad definition of the behavioral sciences: "behavioral sciences refer to the social and biological sciences concerned with the study of behavior"

(Cascio, 2015, p. 348). Regardless of the definition, however, the behavioral sciences encompass a landscape that was far too broad for the committee to examine systematically. It would not have been possible to search the literature for discussion of ontologies in even a fraction of the disciplines that fall under the behavioral umbrella to try to understand how ontologies are developed and used in each of those contexts, or to investigate the particular challenges to ontology development and use in each. The committee, therefore, focused its information gathering on the domain of mental health. We explored issues from this domain in detail in order to develop our thinking about how ontologies function and serve science and to develop conclusions and recommendations that could generalize across the behavioral domain.

Use Cases

Ontologies are not built for their own sake, but rather to serve identified shared goals and concerns about human behavior. We explore these goals and concerns throughout the report, but the foundations for this report are twofold: their basic utility in the behavioral sciences and the concept of "use cases" (cited in the study charge)—a term coined in the context of software engineering to refer to situations in which software is usefully applied or to which it responds.

It is important to distinguish an ontology from its use cases. In simplest terms, a use case is a narrative description or story involving someone interacting with a system to achieve a particular goal (Larman, 2004; Leffingwell and Widrig, 2003). Given the utility of use cases for application design, use case modeling has been highly formalized in software engineering.[4] Use cases are essentially envisioned scenarios (i.e., models) for what a system should do to help someone achieve a goal in a given context. Thus, they are explicitly different from case examples, case studies, or exemplars, which represent fully realized instances of systems or applications.

Use case modeling is a valuable tool for designing an ontology.[5] It is possible to enumerate and illustrate uses cases in terms of five parameters: (1) actors, (2) behaving in a particular context, (3) using a resource, (4) to achieve an expected outcome, (5) that may affect additional stakeholders.[6]

---

[4] For example, the Unified Modeling Language (UML), a widely used graphical language for visualizing, designing, documenting, and building object-based systems, represents use cases as one of its 13 core modeling diagrams.

[5] In the context of evidence-based reasoning, the first step in ontology design typically involves determination of the concepts of interest, which inherently involves envisioning the high-level goals that the ontology will be able to serve within a specific domain with respect to individuals, agents, or organizations with clearly defined roles (Tecuci et al., 2016).

[6] This approach is based on a simplification of the UML methodology described in Randolph (2004).

The committee developed a working formulation of this rubric, using the acronym ACRES: actors, context, resources, expected (outcome), stakeholders. In the context of the behavioral sciences, the resource might be any ontological entity (e.g., a list of concepts and relationships) or ontologically enabled system (e.g., an application that uses an ontology to perform its functions). An example from the biomedical context is the Resource Discovery System (see Tenebaum et al., 2011). The committee's working definitions of the other terms illustrate the relevance of use case modeling for ontology use and development in the behavioral sciences:

- Actor: Anyone (or anything) who performs a behavior to put a demand on the resource or system. Actors can be people, usually identified by roles (e.g., teacher, student, caregiver, scientist), but can also include organizations (e.g., a hospital, a school board), as well as computer systems (e.g., a software application).
- Context: The conditions that must be true or present before the use case proceeds (e.g., in a classroom; at bedtime; all parties using Hindi as their spoken language). The context sets constraints on the use case (and on the relevant ontologies), such that there is no presumption of a universally appropriate ontology, set of terms, concepts, or relationships.
- Resource: Any ontological entity (i.e., an ontology or its components or derivatives) or any system or object that is proximally informed or enabled by an ontological entity (e.g., a visualization tool that illustrates concepts; a knowledge graph; a search engine).
- Expected outcome: The goal state or preferred state of the actor (e.g., to have graduate students learn a fact; to retrieve a local summary of related claims for mental health services)
- Stakeholder: Any individual or entity with vested interests in the behavior of the resource or system under discussion or who may be affected by it. Since many people are stakeholders by virtue of their roles, an individual may have multiple stakeholder identities. Stakeholders may be the actors (e.g., a teacher who might use a resource) or the people who are affected by the action (e.g., the students affected by a teacher's use of the resource).

Box 1-3 presents a list of possible stakeholders to show the broad set of use cases for behavioral science ontologies and ontology resources.

To gain insight into the range of potential use cases for ontologies in the behavioral science, the committee conducted an informal self-survey. Participating committee members enumerated possible use cases, specific ways different actors in a given context could use an ontological resource to achieve expected results relevant to a set of stakeholders. This exercise

> **BOX 1-3**
> **Possible Stakeholders for Behavioral Research**
>
> **Educators and Students:** Faculty, teachers, instructors in educational institutions, from elementary through graduate school, as well as instructors working in other educational contexts such as workshops, online training events, or standalone training institutes, and their students
> **Researchers:** Those whose work involves discovery and knowledge production, often in such settings as universities, industry, or government
> **Policy Makers:** Those whose work involves crafting legislation or guidelines that govern specific industries, professions, or the public
> **Health Care Practitioners:** Those whose work involves providing direct service or the guidance of that service to consumers with behavioral health needs (including providers not involved primarily in mental health care, such as pediatrics, nursing, etc.)
> **Patients and Their Families:** People who use mental health and health care services
> **Public:** People who want to understand behavioral phenomena
> **Administrators:** Individuals who manage the dependencies among resources and activities relevant to behavioral health care, including (but not limited to) insurance plans, school mental health programs, community programming
> **Providers:** Individuals or organizations that design or distribute products relevant to behavioral health

was not a means to model or design specific ontology applications, but simply to assess the potential of behavioral science ontologies to facilitate important goals.[7]

Despite the small sample involved with this exercise, a considerable diversity of use cases emerged; see Appendix B. Researchers were the most commonly cited actors, but health care providers, policy makers, educators, students, administrators, and the general public were also cited. Identified contexts included research workplaces, health care facilities, online or mobile devices, educational institutions, government offices, and homes. Broader contexts were also noted, such as general conditions (e.g., "during a pandemic").

---

[7]The 10 committee members who participated in the self-survey generated 225 data elements across 46 use cases. Use cases followed the ACRES structure, such that any use case could be articulated as a narrative sentence. For example, one use case specified "expert practitioners [actors] in doctors' offices [context] use an ontology of key mental health symptoms and disorders that arise during a pandemic [resource] to improve communication about mental health [expected result] with children and parents [stakeholders]."

Expected results or goals of use cases showed the greatest diversity, including:

- scientific goals (e.g., "theory advancement," "improving methodological rigor," "inform research priorities");
- health-related goals (e.g., "to manage diet," "to obtain guidance on better sleep," "to promote masking or social distancing");
- educational goals (e.g., "to prepare a dissertation," "to improve diagnostically relevant knowledge"); and
- community-focused goals (e.g., "to educate citizens about better managing their own finances," "to empower citizens to resolve situations involving law enforcement," "to learn a new language").

In terms of beneficiaries, the public was the most frequently cited beneficiary of ontological resources but researchers, health care recipients, students, administrators, health care providers, policy makers, and educators were also noted.

Although this was not a formal investigation, it suggested the diversity of applications of behavioral science ontologies and the importance of ontologies to both actors and beneficiaries not directly involved in science. The committee considered these results a useful standard of comparison for behavioral science ontologies currently in existence—how existing ontologies serve the potential range of use cases it is possible to imagine.

STUDY PROCESS: FOUR KEY QUESTIONS

The committee recognized that some scholars and stakeholders may question the value of developing and using ontologies in the behavioral sciences, while others have high aspirations for their potential benefits. We began our work from an agnostic stance, eager to better understand how ontologies have actually operated in the behavioral sciences, the challenges of developing and sustaining ontologies in this context, and the possibilities they offer for supporting advances in behavioral research. Developing our conclusions and recommendations did not require the committee to take a position on ontology-related controversies in the behavioral sciences, but rather to assess the available evidence to determine how increased attention to ontologies could advance work in this domain. This report provides our answers to four basic questions:

- Why do ontologies matter?
- What exactly are ontologies?

- How do ontologies facilitate science?
- How can the engineering of ontologies in the behavioral sciences be strengthened?

Although the study charge specifies the behavioral sciences, we note that many, if not most of the committee's answers to these questions, and our conclusions and recommendations, apply beyond the behavioral domain.

Answering these four questions required investigation of methods, philosophy of science, and ontology development and use cases, in addition to analysis of existing evidence about the impacts of behavioral ontologies. The committee sought to understand the conceptual issues that pertain to ontologies, regardless of the mechanisms by which they are developed, and also to understand in detail how technological innovations have influenced the way behavioral ontologies are developed and used. We examined how ontologies themselves have been studied, the history of ontology use in the behavioral sciences, useful examples from other domains, identifiable characteristics or patterns in the ontologies that have proved effective and sustainable, and the challenges that developers and users of ontologies encounter.

The two primary sources of information we could review were (1) published research about individual ontologies or about the role of ontologies and their development and use, both in science in general and in the behavioral sciences, and (2) investigation of example ontologies in the behavioral sciences and related fields. As we will discuss, particularly in Chapters 3 and 5, existing ontologies and related knowledge structures in the behavioral sciences vary in significant ways and are not easily counted or categorized, but there are fewer ontologies in the behavioral domain than in other scientific domains. Thus, the examples we explored are those that are well known or important for varied reasons, rather than a systematically derived sample.

The committee held two public workshops at which invited experts presented information about individual example ontologies and offered historical and philosophical perspectives on their role in the behavioral sciences.[8] We reviewed published literature and commissioned five papers to deepen our understanding of a range of topics:[9] see Box 1-4. Subgroups of the committee also held structured discussions with experts about key issues. The workshops and papers allowed us to look closely at example ontologies that reflected a range of contexts; we refer to them throughout the report.

---

[8] The workshop agendas and presentations are available on the project website, at https://www.nationalacademies.org/our-work/accelerating-social-and-behavioral-science-through-ontology-development-and-use

[9] The commissioned papers are available at https://nap.nationalacademies.org/catalog/26464/ontologies-in-the-behavioral-sciences-accelerating-research-and-the-spread

> **BOX 1-4**
> **Papers Commissioned by the Committee**
>
> Ontological Issues in Patient Reported Outcomes: Conceptual issues and challenges addressed by the Patient-Reported Outcomes Measurement Information System (PROMIS®)
>
>   **David Cella and Ronald Hays**
>
> Key Issues in the Development of the ICD and Its Effects on Medicine
>
>   **Christopher Chute**
>
> Formal Representation of Ontologies for Automation of Analyses
>
>   **Janna Hastings**
>
> Scoping Review of Ontologies in the Behavioral Sciences
>
>   **Louise Falzon**
>
> Problems and Solutions in the Implementation of Integrative Pluralism in Psychiatric Genetics Research
>
>   **Kenneth Kendler**

These sources provided valuable information and insights but, as we discuss in Chapter 5, the existing literature did not offer empirical answers to many of our questions. In order to provide a response to this important study charge that could be useful now, the committee deliberated and arrived at judgments based on the information available. The committee met formally five times, once in person, and also collaborated using Zoom and other technologies throughout the process of digesting the information and developing the report.

GUIDE TO THIS REPORT

The report is structured by the committee's four questions, listed above. It begins, in Chapter 2, with a look at why ontologies are important in the first place: the scientific problems an ontology can address, the relationship between those problems and challenges in translating behavioral research into practice that can improve health and alleviate suffering, and the ways stakeholders are affected by those challenges. Chapter 3 provides a technical and detailed discussion of what an ontology is, in the context of the behavioral sciences. Chapter 4 explores how ontologies can advance scientific progress in the behavioral sciences. In Chapter 5 we turn to the question of how ontologies could be used more effectively in the behavioral sciences, beginning with an overview of what is known about existing ones and then exploring the components needed to engineer ontologies. The report closes in Chapter 6 with an overview of the committee's primary conclusions about the development and use of ontologies, and recommendations for supporting and sustaining efforts to more fully integrate ontologies in the behavioral sciences. Appendix A provides basic information about example ontologies referred to in this report; Appendix B lists the example use cases generated in a committee self-survey; and Appendix C provides biographical sketches of the committee members and staff.

REFERENCES

Adhikari, D. (2016). Exploring the differences between social and behavioral science. *Behavioral Development Bulletin, 21*(2), 128–135. https://doi.org/10.1037/bdb0000029

Bellido, A., Ruisoto, P., Beltran-Velasco, A., and Clemente-Suárez, V.J. (2018). State of the art on the use of portable digital devices to assess stress in humans. *Journal of Medical Systems, 42*(6), 100. https://doi.org/10.1007/s10916-018-0955-0

Blair, A. (2010). *Too Much to Know: Managing Scholarly Information Before the Modern Age.* New Haven, CT: Yale University Press.

Cascio, W.F. (2015). Human resource management, psychology of. In J. Wright (Ed.), *International Encyclopedia of the Social & Behavioral Sciences* (2nd ed.), 348–352. https://doi.org/10.1016/B978-0-08-097086-8.73024-8

Cella, D., and Hays, R. (2021). *Ontological Issues in Patient Reported Outcomes: Conceptual Issues and Challenges Addressed by the Patient-Reported Outcomes Measurement Information System (PROMIS®).* Commissioned paper prepared for the Committee on Accelerating Behavioral Science Through Ontology Development and Use, National Academies of Sciences, Engineering, and Medicine. Available: https://nap.nationalacademies.org/resource/26464/Cella-and-Hays-comissioned-paper.pdf

Chute, C. (2021). *Key Issues in the Development of the ICD and Its Effects on Medicine.* Commissioned paper prepared for the Committee on Accelerating Behavioral Science Through Ontology Development and Use, National Academies of Sciences, Engineering, and Medicine. Available: https://nap.nationalacademies.org/resource/26464/Chute-commissioned-paper.pdf.

Crosswell, A.D., and Lockwood, K.G. (2020). Best practices for stress measurement: How to measure psychological stress in health research. *Health Psychology Open, 7*(2), 2055102920933072. https://doi.org/10.1177/2055102920933072

Diderot, D., and Alembert, J.L.R. (2001). *L'encyclopédie die Diderot et d'Alembert.* Paris: Inter-Livres.

du Plessis, L., Škunca, N., and Dessimoz, C. (2011). The what, where, how and why of gene ontology—a primer for bioinformaticians. *Briefings in Bioinformatics, 12*(6), 723–735. https://doi.org/10.1093/bib/bbr002

Editors of Encyclopaedia Britannica. (n.d.). Behavioral science. *Encyclopaedia Britannica.* https://www.britannica.com/science/behavioral-science

Falzon, L. (2021). *Scoping Review of Ontologies in the Behavioral Sciences.* Commissioned paper prepared for the Committee on Accelerating Behavioral Science Through Ontology Development and Use, National Academies of Sciences, Engineering, and Medicine. Available: https://nap.nationalacademies.org/resource/26464/Falzon-comissioned-paper.pdf

The Gene Ontology Consortium. (2019). The Gene Ontology resource: 20 years and still GOing strong. *Nucleic Acids Research, 47*, D331-D338. https://doi.org/10.1093/nar/gky1055

Gruber, T.R. (1995). Toward principles for the design of ontologies used for knowledge sharing? *International Journal of Human-Computer Studies, 43*(5-6), 907–928. Available: https://doi.org/10.1006/ijhc.1995.1081

Hastings, J. (2021). *Formal Representations of Ontologies for Automation of Analyses*. Commissioned paper prepared for the Committee on Accelerating Behavioral Science Through Ontology Development and Use, National Academies of Sciences, Engineering, and Medicine. Available: https://nap.nationalacademies.org/resource/26464/Hastings-comissioned-paper.pdf

Hodos, W., and Campbell, C.B.G. (1969). Scala naturae: Why there is no theory in comparative psychology. *Psychological Review, 76*(4), 337–350. Available: https://doi.org/10.1037/h0027523

Kendler, K.S. (2021). *Problems and Solutions in the Implementation of Integrative Pluralism in Psychiatric Genetics Research*. Commissioned paper prepared for the Committee on Accelerating Behavioral Science Through Ontology Development and Use, National Academies of Sciences, Engineering, and Medicine. Available: https://nap.nationalacademies.org/resource/26464/Kendler-comissioned-paper.pdf

Larman, C. (2004). *Apply UML and Patterns: An Introduction to Object-Oriented Analysis and Design and the Unified Process*. https://personal.utdallas.edu/~chung/SP/applying-uml-and-patterns.pdf

Leffingwell, D., and Widrig, D. (2003). *Managing Software Requirements: A Use Case Approach* (2nd ed.). Boston, MA: Addison-Wesley.

Michie, S., Thomas, J., Johnston, M., Aonghusa, P. M., Shawe-Taylor, J., Kelly, M. P., Deleris, L. A., Finnerty, A. N., Marques, M. M., Norris, E., O'Mara-Eves, A., and West, R. (2017). The Human Behaviour-Change Project: Harnessing the power of artificial intelligence and machine learning for evidence synthesis and interpretation. *Implementation Science, 12*(1), 121. https://doi.org/10.1186/s13012-017-0641-5

NASEM (National Academies of Sciences, Engineering, and Medicine). (2019). *Fostering Healthy Mental, Emotional, and Behavioral Development in Children and Youth*. Washington, DC: National Academies Press. https://doi.org/10.17226/25201

Poldrack, R.A., Kittur, A., Kalar, D., Miller, E., Seppa, C., Gil, Y., Parker, D.S., Sabb, F.W., and Bilder, R.M. (2011). The Cognitive Atlas: Toward a knowledge foundation for cognitive neuroscience. *Frontiers in Neuroinformatics, 5*, 17. https://doi.org/10.3389/fninf.2011.00017

Randolph, G. (2004). Use-cases and personas: A case study in light-weight user interaction design for small development projects. *Information Science, 4*, 105–116. https://doi.org/10.28945/505

Simon, H.A. (1971). Designing organizations for an information-rich world. In M. Greenberger (Ed.), *Computers, Communications, and the Public Interest*, 37–52. Baltimore, MD: Johns Hopkins University Press.

Tecuci, G., Marcu, D., Boicu, M., and Schum, D.A. (2016). *Knowledge Engineering: Building Cognitive Assistants for Evidence-Based Reasoning*. Cambridge, U.K.: Cambridge University Press.

Tenenbaum, J.D., Whetzel, P.L., Anderson, K., Borromeo, C.D., Dinov, I.D., Gabriel, D., Kirschner, B., Mirel, B., Morris, T., Noy, N., Nyulas, C., Rubenson, D., Saxman, P.R., Singh, H., Whelan, N., Wright, Z., Athey, B.D., Becich, M.J., Ginsburg, G.S., Musen, M.A., Smith, K.A., Tarantal, A.F., Rubin, D.L., and Lyster, P. (2011). The Biomedical Resource Ontology (BRO) to enable resource discovery in clinical and translational research. *Journal of Biomedical Informatics, 44*(1), 137–145. https://doi.org/10.1016/j.jbi.2010.10.003

Wolman, B.B. (Eds.). (1989). *Dictionary of Behavioral Science* (2nd ed.). Cambridge, MA: Academic Press.

2

Why Ontologies Matter

Why worry about behavioral ontologies, when scientists and those who apply scientific knowledge may have many other pressing concerns? To understand why this seemingly arcane idea is so important, it is helpful to consider what problems arise when ontologies are not in place. For example, imagine a mental health professional who treats adolescents in a practice where productivity demands are high. This professional knows there is a wealth of research related to their work but struggles to identify answers to specific questions that arise in the course of their practice. With very limited time to keep up with journals that document the latest research findings, health care providers just want to be able to determine what evidence-based treatment approaches are new and relevant, which ones could help their patients, and how their patients might respond to these approaches. Seeking answers in the literature, they usually encounter a bewildering array of ideas, measures, and treatments.

Researchers have developed many terms and models for studying mental health disorders, as well as possible treatments. But that evidence about research developments exists in thousands of research papers published every month, which may be classified in varying ways and venues, using a wide array of possible search terms. A review of 435 randomized clinical trials for youth mental health interventions, for instance, noted that nearly 60 percent of studies (i.e., 258 of the 435) did not use a diagnosis to describe the participants (Chorpita et al., 2011). Instead, many used cutoffs on scales or other criteria to define the study samples (e.g., elevated depression scores, juvenile justice involvement). Even among the minority of trials that reported diagnoses to define their study samples, multiple systems were used, including three different editions of the Diagnostic and Statistical Manual of Mental Disorders (DSM) as well as the International Classification of Diseases (ICD) 10. Other trials reported diagnosis with no specification of the diagnostic classification system used.

If one wishes to retrieve and consider even a nearly complete list of all clinical trials relevant to an adolescent with a diagnosed DSM-5 major depressive disorder, for instance, the task is nearly impossible without a strategy to link the inconsistent definitions of depression. Detecting patterns across the 65 depression-relevant clinical trials (e.g., "effective treatments used with younger depressed youth tend to have these features...") would similarly require a shared conceptualization of the variables of interest from those trials along which inferences were of interest (i.e., how treatments operations were defined, how age was defined) to allow some statistical aggregation. Thus, it is difficult for anyone to draw on an established and evolving evidence base relevant to this particular domain. Although this example highlights the predicament of a busy mental health professional, researchers and others seeking literature relevant to many kinds of questions in many domains routinely face similar dilemmas.

Another sort of ontological problem can be found in the large and rapidly growing literature on the profound ways that disparities affecting population groups defined largely by race and ethnicity influence human health and development throughout people's life spans (see, e.g., Institute of Medicine, 2003, 2012; NASEM, 2019a, 2021). Researchers and members of the general public who are interested in these issues must rely on racial categories used in the collection of data about specified groups.[1] Yet the accuracy of the available data depends on the validity of the way those groups have been labelled. Most early scientific efforts to classify and understand groups of human beings in this way are now recognized as both misguided and harmful, and the definitions have evolved continuously over time (National Research Council, 2004): see Box 2-1. Many recent studies of racial and ethnic groups are based on the understanding that these are evolving, socially constructed categories—not biological ones—and so the earlier data must be interpreted carefully (see, e.g., Hunley et al., 2016; National Research Council, 2004). On a purely practical level, researchers studying trends that affect population groups need to account for changes over time in the definitions of who was in which group.

There are no easy answers for challenges such as these, but they partly reflect limitations in the way ontologies—basic tools for communicating clearly about concepts and constructs, and the way they are classified—are used, or not used, in the behavioral sciences (see Box 2-2).

---

[1] The committee gathered valuable insights about these issues from a session at their first workshop; see https://www.nationalacademies.org/event/06-29-2021/understanding-ontologies-in-context-workshop-2

> **BOX 2-1**
> **Racial Categories Used in the U.S. Census**
>
> Much behavioral and social science research relies on U.S. census counts of population groups. When the first census was taken, in 1790, there were three categories: (1) free White males or free White females, (2) all other free persons, and (3) slaves (Pew Research Center, 2020). The census categories have changed with almost every census in the years since then. In 2020, individuals completing the census could select from among 17 racial and ethnic categories, select "other," select more than one, or write in a category. These categories—the names assigned to groups of interest—have reflected changing social and political realities, not scientific ones. Nevertheless, because census data is essential to many kinds of research, these categories are integral to the study of phenomena in which behavioral scientists, and society, are deeply interested.

In this chapter we look first at the most visible challenges: the reasons ontologies can make a difference in people's lives, including synthesizing and applying the knowledge produced by scientists. We then turn to the scientific challenges that underlie these problems, looking first at difficulties with generalizing about scientific findings and then at challenges with building and structuring knowledge.

> **BOX 2-2**
> **Concepts, Constructs, and Classes**
>
> Researchers use the terms *concept* and *construct* to refer to behavioral or psychological phenomena—such as memory, anger, decision making, or attention—that have been observed empirically (as distinguished from reference to such ideas in everyday speech). A *concept* is the basic definition of an abstract notion, the representation of an entity, or a group of entities. Scientists define concepts as *constructs* in crafting hypotheses or identifying specific phenomena to be measured or observed. For example, a concept for depression is the list of symptoms (i.e., features) used to diagnose the disorder. This concept is often used as a construct (perhaps defined more precisely) in research on depression, to guide subject selection, measurement (e.g., in surveys that assess depression symptoms), and the inferences made from data. Scientists (and others) arrange groups of entities or phenomena—objects, events, or individuals—in *classes* that are regarded as similar in some way for some purpose, such as studying the features of a disease to improve diagnosis and treatment (Murphy, 2002). For depression, a class might be a set of persons experiencing depression symptoms. We note that in the context of cognitive science, the term *category* is used to denote groups of entities with similar features but that *category* is used in a different mathematical sense in the context of ontologies, where *class* is used for such groups. The committee uses *class* and *classification* for this report.

CHALLENGES WITH SYNTHESIZING AND APPLYING KNOWLEDGE

Behavioral scientists produce a vast amount of research every year, but the publication of the results is only an initial step in the process by which scientific knowledge can bring benefits to society. For new knowledge to benefit patients; clinicians, investigators; and professionals in education, business, law, and other domains, it has to be tested and reproduced, and the findings have to be managed, synthesized, disseminated, and applied. Without ontologies, all of these functions are more difficult.

Conscientious scholars and clinical practitioners are expected to keep abreast of literature in their field. But is this expectation realistic? Every year, there are 23,000 scientific journals that collectively publish more than 2 million peer-reviewed scientific articles each year (Elsevier, 2020; National Science Board, National Science Foundation, 2021). In the United States alone, an estimated 422,000 papers were published in 2018. No human being could sift through the volume of literature relevant to even a single domain to retrieve the information they need to stay current or identify nuances and trends in research findings.

An estimate of the rate of science growth since the mid-1600s, based on data from the Web of Science and the number of cited references identified per year, illustrates the scope of the challenge: see Figure 2-1. Acceleration has been most rapid over the last 70 years, with the greatest inflection within the most recent decade; there are no signs the trend will decelerate (Bornmann and Mutz, 2014).

Most academics and health care providers can devote only a limited number of hours to reading the scientific literature in their fields. Academics must teach, participate in university service activities, advise students, and engage in community service. Clinical practitioners spend most of their time seeing patients, writing notes, dealing with insurance issues, and managing their practices. That leaves them little time to survey, let alone consume, the literally thousands of potentially relevant articles that enter the literature each year.[2] Without ontologies to frame the scientific discourse, it is practically impossible for stakeholders to reliably identify the most important developments in their fields.

One illustration of challenges facing the behavioral sciences was provided by a recent historical review of 50 years of randomized clinical trials on the subject of youth mental health (Okamura et al., 2020). The authors found that the way the studies were classified—their implicit ontological structures—did not offer clear guidance for enhancing the delivery of care.

Treatment manuals that specify the nature of a clinical intervention have long been used as the written codifications of psychotherapy procedures

---

[2] See Kim et al. (2020) for a discussion of searching academic literature in the internet age.

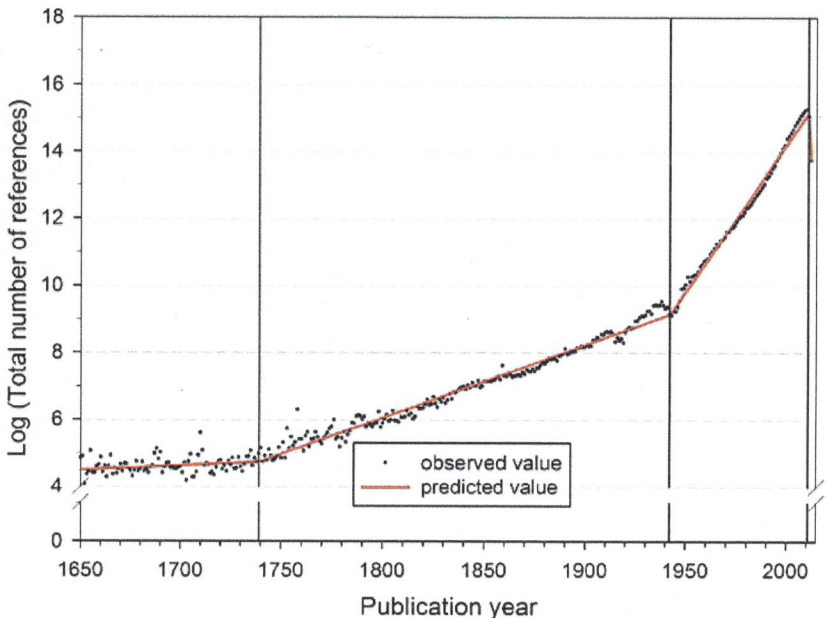

FIGURE 2-1 Growth in the annual number of cited references from 1650 to 2012.
SOURCE: Bornmann and Mutz (2014, p. 2218).

to be used. Such manuals have served as a tool for defining different approaches being studied in clinical research trials.[3] In their review, Okamura and colleagues (2020) compared this dominant conceptualization of treatments based on manuals to a less widely used way of classifying intervention approaches, in which it is the component practices defined within these manuals, known as "practice elements," that are classified (Chorpita et al., 2005). Practice elements include specific procedures typically enumerated in a manual, such as guiding caregivers in the use of a reward program, teaching a problem-solving technique to a youth, or promoting specific communication skills among family members. Such procedures are typically used across many instances of evidence-based programs for youth and family mental health (e.g., Chorpita and Daleiden, 2009). The relationship between practice elements and manuals is basically one of component membership. Although they include other material, manuals are collections

---

[3] Building on earlier policy recommendations from the American Psychological Association Task Force on Promotion and Dissemination of Psychological Procedures, for example, Chambless et al. (1998, p. 6) argued that " . . . brand names [labels] are not the critical identifiers [of an intervention]. The manuals are."

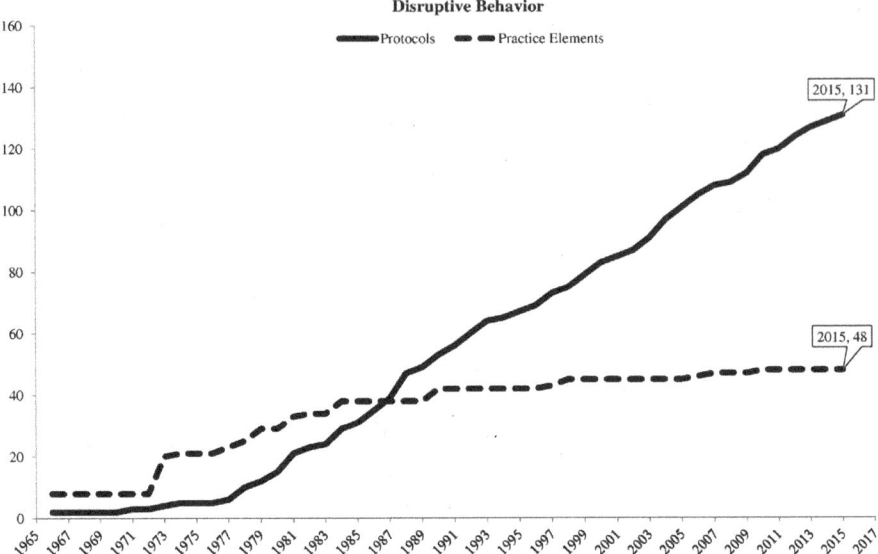

FIGURE 2-2 Disruptive behavior protocols and practice element frequencies over time.
SOURCE: Okamura et al. (2020, p. 75).

of practice elements, in the same way that a playlist represents a collection of songs.

Figure 2-2 shows the proliferation of treatment manuals (referred to as "protocols" in the figure), especially over the last 25 years (Chorpita and Daleiden, 2014, p. 329). By 2015, 131 protocols targeting disruptive behavior in youth had been tested in 149 randomized clinical trials (Okamura et al., 2020). In contrast, a smaller number of practice elements, only 48, appeared in these manuals, with a slope that is clearly shallower over the latter half of the period.[4]

As the example illustrates, many new manuals have been developed and tested, but these manuals largely appear to be new combinations of existing practice elements, rather than conceptually distinctive approaches to intervention. Returning to the playlist metaphor: although the field is producing many new playlists, they appear mostly to be combinations of the same set

---

[4] The same data source used by Okamura et al. (2020), PWEBS [see https://www.practicewise.com/#services], shows that as of November 2021, there are 304 manuals using 58 of the practice elements specified in the analysis by Okamura and colleagues, which, if superimposed on their figure, shows an increasing separation between the rate of innovation of clinical procedures and the full protocols tested in trials.

of songs. In other words, despite decades of research regarding psychosocial treatments for disruptive behavior, the actual protocols used in real-world practice are rarely innovative, and there is little truly systematic development and refinement across protocols and approaches. Moreover, detailed reviews of actual clinical care have shown that the component procedures of these treatments are typically delivered irregularly, with systematic omissions, and at low levels of intensity and fidelity (Kazdin, 2018; Garland et al., 2010). It has been difficult to perceive this lack of progress because of the ways the field describes and classifies the elements being studied. A lack of ontological clarity makes it difficult to perceive significant trends and highlight valuable developing knowledge about effective combinations of practice elements.

The significant point is not that one conceptualization of the interventions is superior to the other. There clearly was and is a need for both views: specification of entire treatments as collections of procedures with defined length, pace, order, and other features, on one hand, and specification of the subordinate common elements of the treatments studied on the other hand. Although both conceptualizations are important, a more granular "elements" approach allows synthesis of a wealth of interventions that otherwise could be difficult to aggregate, and thereby can lend itself to particular use cases. What is important is that the way that entities are labeled and classified has implications for synthesis and retrievability.

This example also illustrates two key challenges that are relevant to most, if not all, areas of behavioral science. The first is the potential for inefficiency of ongoing research. For example, without an ontology that explicitly specifies relationships among different entities within a domain, researchers run the risk of engaging in empirically or conceptually siloed retesting of the same research questions. In this example, it would mean repeatedly testing whether similar collections of roughly equivalent clinical procedures performed better than a control group in a randomized trial. Although it is possible that the past 20 years shown in Figure 2-2 underrepresent some types of innovation, such as how the same clinical procedures were potentially rearranged or re-sequenced, the ability to visualize that innovation depends on having explicit specification of practice elements or procedures and of the ways they are arranged for application; the latter is especially underdeveloped or absent in most areas of behavioral science (Chorpita and Daleiden, 2014, p. 330). This challenge is not unique to intervention research or to mental health; it arises from a fundamental challenge with synthesizing an evidence base using a shared, explicit specification of the concepts underlying research in a specified area (i.e., an ontology).

The second challenge is a manifestation of the more general and ubiquitous "wealth of information" problem, that as a body of knowledge grows, its retrievability and actionability decreases (Simon, 1971). Research in the behavioral sciences is producing a body of knowledge so extensive that it is increasingly difficult to apply efficiently and effectively. As the example above illustrates, it is unlikely that without an ontology, the more than 300 treatment programs tested in clinicaltrials.gov could be organized effectively to guide service delivery for a mental health care provider. Roughly 50 years ago Herbert Simon (1971) provided an aspirational description of science as "the process of replacing unordered masses of brute fact with tidy statements of orderly relations from which these facts can be inferred" (p. 45). However, identification of patterns and distillation of facts both depend on the ability to aggregate, filter, and otherwise manage the evidence, which is currently limited in the behavioral sciences. In short, ontologies make it much easier to filter, aggregate, synthesize, and retrieve very large knowledge bases that would otherwise be too complex to be fully useable—and to generalize that knowledge.

CHALLENGES WITH GENERALIZING RESEARCH FINDINGS

Questions about the robustness of research in the social and behavioral sciences have attracted significant attention over the last two decades. This issue came to public attention in 2013 when questions about the replicability of a wide range of papers were raised in both the academic and popular literatures. In response, an expert committee from the National Science Foundation (NSF) considered the problem of robust science in the behavioral, social, and economic sciences (Bollen et al., 2015).[5] The report drew attention to problems with the orderly development of knowledge, including the indiscriminate use of methods and measures to evaluate constructs without careful documentation of the relation between the measures and the constructs to be measured. The report identified generalizability as a serious problem in the behavioral sciences. Ideally, researchers hope to design studies that yield results that are equivalently applicable across different sets of study participants and can be generalized to apply much more broadly. Problems with generalizability can arise from a number of factors, several of which are relevant to a potential role for ontologies. One difficulty is in generalizing results obtained using a particular method or measure to other contexts or populations where different methods or measures of the same constructs were used. As we discuss below, the challenge of identifying comparable measures for phenomena is in part an ontological one.

Another challenge is that a causal or predictive association may be found in one population or set of circumstances (e.g., predominantly White

---

[5] A recent report addresses issues of reproducibility and replicability in science more generally (NASEM, 2019b).

undergraduate students at a large state university) but not in others (e.g., Black adults in Chicago), even if the same measures are used. In such cases it may be unclear what conclusion to draw. Perhaps there was some sort of critical flaw or limitation in the original study. Alternatively, perhaps the original study was valid for the study population but there are additional, unrecognized moderating or contextual variables that affect other populations differently. Another possibility is that although the results from the original study were replicable under the same laboratory conditions, they were formulated in terms of treatments and measures rarely present in real-world settings. Ontologies that define the entities that are important in a field of study will support the development of measures and research designs that can be replicated and generalized.

Ultimately, problems with generalizability create difficulties for consumers of research—whether other researchers, health care providers, or other stakeholders. Ontologies can help by providing a framework for accurately describing and comparing conclusions, describing how measures are related to conclusions, identifying moderating variables, and distinguishing domains or regimes in which relationships hold from those in which they do not.

CHALLENGES WITH BUILDING AND STRUCTURING KNOWLEDGE

It is a basic function of science to label and classify the phenomena that are observed and organize them for study in a particular domain. Scientific classifications are the basis for the organization of knowledge through the formation of hypotheses, the design of experiments, the modeling and interpretation of data, and the integration of findings. Clear labeling is the basis for systems of classification, such as ontologies, but even in situations in which there is no sanctioned one, scientists still rely on classification (grouping of phenomena). When this classification is approached formally, the resulting classifications may be ontologies (see Chapter 3). Often, however, it proceeds more automatically and implicitly, as when so-called folk categories from everyday life (informal understandings of phenomena, such as cognition, emotion, perception) play an unrecognized role in behavioral science.

As a relatively young group of disciplines, the behavioral sciences are still developing and refining many of the sets of concepts and classifications on which they are based (and by which each organizes the knowledge that is created), as well as the constructs useful for scientific study. And the challenge of discerning whether two constructs actually describe the same entity or phenomenon has been an issue in the behavioral sciences for more than a century (Larsen and Bong, 2016). In general, the constructs and classifications that have been established in the behavioral sciences have not been systematized (see, e.g., Davis et al., 2015; Barrett, 2009; Lilienfeld et al., 2015; Lawson and Robbins, 2021). Scientists working within even a narrow field may use different constructs and classifications for the same phenomena depending on their interests and other factors. They may be using the same word (label) for a phenomenon or a class and not recognize that they are actually referring to different phenomena or classes. Indeed, the charge given to this committee reflects an understanding that a broad range of stakeholders are interested in the continuing development and refinement of how behavioral science knowledge is organized and disseminated. We briefly review some of the challenges associated with classification and with defining and measuring constructs that point to a need for greater reliance on ontologies.

Challenges with Classification

Definitions of many of the concepts, constructs, and classifications used in the behavioral sciences may not be widely shared. As already noted, scientists identify classes by focusing on certain features of equivalence (features that the entities or instances are thought to share), but these groupings do not necessarily correspond to the words that label them in principled and consistent ways. As a result, scientists and science consumers may not easily recognize the extent to which two entities or even two constructs are similar or different. Even when a classification system is accepted within a domain of study, it may be inadequate or unsuitable for its intended purpose.

In addition, classifications inevitably become out of date as scientific knowledge evolves in response to new findings and new ideas. For example, Linnaeus, the legendary taxonomist, classified rabies as a mental illness because end-stage rabies results in confusion, agitation, and hallucinations (Linné and Schröder, 1763, cited in Chute, 2021). Linnaeus created the class before the infectious origins of rabies were understood. A more contemporary illustration is the 11th edition of the International Classification of Diseases (ICD), which significantly modified its classification of mental health disorders to reflect current understanding of pathology, setting aside many terms that are rooted in Freudian psychoanalysis (Chute, 2021): see Box 2-3.

A classification that has not been developed systematically might not be useful and may even be counterproductive. For example, in the mental health field, diagnosis often involves placing individuals into discrete classes. Yet, evidence challenges the reliability of many psychological and psychiatric diagnoses (Regier et al., 2013). Furthermore, mental health diagnoses and the symptoms that underlie them are highly intercorrelated.

> **BOX 2-3**
> **The International Classification of Diseases (ICD)**
>
> The ICD is recognized as perhaps the largest effort ever to list and name medical conditions, though Hippocrates may have been the first to describe a science-based theory of disease, in the 4th century, BC. It built on ideas that gained momentum during the 19th century, including Florence Nightingale's call for a definitive list of causes of morbidity and mortality. In 1900, an international conference launched the plan for what became the ICD, which was subsequently taken over by the World Health Organization. The ICD is updated regularly; the 11th edition (ICD-11) is the most recent major revision, released in 2019.
>
> More than 1,000 experts were involved in revising just the mental health component of ICD-11, which proposes new strategies rather than simply clarifying and expanding previous classifications. The experts involved in the process sought to align diagnostic guidelines with the ways clinicians in practice conceptualize psychopathology and to respond to the challenge of new scientific work that is inconsistent with terms and classifications in earlier editions of the ICD. For example, gender identity concerns are no longer classified as mental health problems, and the new edition includes a chapter on sexual health. ICD-11 also adopts a lifespan approach, replacing the traditional model of studying childhood and adulthood as separate life stages.
>
> SOURCE: Adapted from Chute (2021).

For example, mental disorientation may be associated with several different diagnoses. And disorientation may be highly correlated with other symptoms, such as flat affect, hallucinations, and social distrust. These findings challenge the clinical practice of placing individuals into a primary diagnosis class (Lahey, 2021). The mechanisms that cause a person to display particular signs or symptoms of conduct may vary across individuals.

There are different ways to create classification systems. The most common approach uses collaborative consensus building to define groupings in the observed domain. Empirical statistical methodologies have the potential to support this effort by identifying data that are more or less similar. The statistical approach builds on the estimated correlations between observations and constructs and can sharpen definitions of classes and improve the reliability of an ontology. By identifying correlations among diagnoses and symptoms, for example, it may be possible to replace binary mental health diagnoses (e.g., normal or abnormal) with estimates of where individuals fall along multiple continua (Lahey, 2021; Lahey et al, 2017). This point is discussed further in Chapter 5.

The Jingle Problem

One common problem in the behavioral sciences occurs when researchers assume that two groups of entities that can be distinguished by their features (i.e., they should be considered as two different constructs) are assumed to be the same because they are named by the same word. This is called the jingle problem or fallacy (see, e.g., Kelley, 1927; Gonzalez et al., 2021).[6] An example of the jingle problem is evident in the scientific use of the word "control" and its associated constructs. The same word can refer to the subjective experience of being in control, a feeling of agency or effort, and can also refer to the function of systems or mechanisms that guide behavior (Helmholtz, 1925; Bargh, 1994). Yet there is clear and consistent evidence that the two need not correspond (e.g., Barrett et al., 2004). Similarly, scientists who study emotion often use the same words to refer to a range of very different constructs (see, e.g., Barrett et al., 2019, Fig. 1).

The Jangle Problem

A related problem occurs when scientists assume that two similar phenomena are different because they go by different names. This is called the jangle problem or alternatively, the "toothbrush problem." (so named because behavioral scientists often avoid using others' theories just as people are repulsed by the thought of using others' toothbrushes) (Mischel, 2008). Examples abound in the behavioral sciences. "Coping," "emotion regulation," "self-regulation," and "self-control," or even "cognitive control" may all refer to similar phenomena that share many features. It is possible, of course, that differences in language may indicate subtle but critical differences in the features that scientists focus on when studying and conceptualizing a classification. Nevertheless, it is indisputable that the jangle or toothbrush problem has interfered with the accumulation of knowledge in the behavioral sciences. The proliferation of measures and theories often leads to more confusion than clarification.

Challenges with Defining Constructs

The jingle and jangle problems highlight the importance of clear definitions of constructs. When the same constructs are described by different names or are measured using different instruments, or when different definitions are adopted for the same construct, it hinders scientific communication and clinical application, as well as dissemination.

Consider a relatively straightforward example: the diagnosis of hypertension. Professional organizations have different thresholds for the diag-

---

[6] The terms jingle and jangle are widely accepted in the context of the behavioral sciences but other terms for these problems are used in other scientific disciplines.

nosis of this chronic health condition. According to the American Heart Association and the American College of Cardiology, a 60-year-old man whose blood pressure is 135/87 mmHg has stage one hypertension and is very near the threshold for the most severe level or stage two hypertension (Goetsch, 2021). However, according to the European Society on Hypertension, his blood pressure is high normal (Williams et al., 2018). Moreover, these thresholds have also changed over time. Such differences have consequences. When the guideline from the American College of Cardiology and the American Heart Association lowered the threshold for high blood pressure to >130/80 mmHg, the number of people eligible for treatment increased by 7.5 million, and 13.9 million people became candidates for treatment intensification (Khera et al., 2018).

The situation with hypertension is actually a simple case. Hypertension research uses clearly delineated and widely shared methods and measurement requirements. Blood pressure has a common label, meaning, and causal relationship to other medical conditions. The literature contains several thousand studies that use these common labels, measures, and meanings to empirically validate or refute the hypothesized relationships.

In contrast, the classification of mental health problems presents problems of definition as well as other challenges. Some of these challenges arise from the fact that mental disorders, like many health conditions, are not binary. In defining high blood pressure, epidemiologists and cardiologists identify cut points on the basis of epidemiological studies and expert judgment. Although errors in blood pressure assessment do occur (Padwal et al., 2019), measurement of mental disorders such as depression is inherently less precise and reliable. In addition, there is no clear agreement among investigators and clinicians regarding when to initiate treatment for depression (or other mood disorders). Some experts believe that treatment should be reserved for those who meet diagnostic criteria for a "major" depressive disorder, which frequently is defined as having at least five of the symptoms listed on the Patient Health Questionnaire-9 (Kroenke et al., 2001). But other experts recommend treatment for people with "subsyndromal depression," which is defined as having as few as two symptoms measured by the same instrument. Recent evidence suggests that the point prevalence of subsyndromal depression is about 2.5 times the rate of major depression (Oh et al., 2020) and that most adults would be eligible for a diagnosis of subsyndromal depression at some point in their lives (Rapaport and Judd, 1998).

Challenges with Measuring Constructs

In almost all areas of science, a distinction is drawn between a phenomenon and the measures used to observe and assess its features. That is, scientists recognize that any measure may be a less than perfectly precise representation of what is being measured. In some areas of science, there are recognized ways of measuring the same phenomena that consistently yield the same results. Obtaining consistent results from a number of different measures is often taken to be strong evidence both that the phenomenon in question is real or robust and that the measures themselves are reliable and valid. Yet the availability of multiple measures has not always enhanced progress in the behavioral sciences.

For example, the jingle problem often appears when measures that go by the same name (i.e., are supposed to be measures of the same construct) do not correlate. In the domain of emotion, self-reports of experience; observations of facial, body, and vocal behaviors; and physiological measurements for any given emotional constructs (anger, fear, happiness, etc.) correlate weakly with one another, or sometimes not at all. There are many possible reasons for a lack of correlation among measures: one or more of the measures may be defective in some way; the different measures may be measuring features that differ in some subtle way; the entity (i.e., instance of emotion) being measured may be heterogeneous in unrecognized ways; or the constructs in question may have a relational, contextual meaning that varies across its instances (see, e.g., Bollen and Lennox, 1991; Barrett, 2011). But it does highlight the importance of careful attention to measures and their assumed relationships to the constructs they are used to assess; lack of agreement, although frustrating, can be a source of information about the nature of the phenomena being studied.

Another example of the jingle problem in measurement can be seen in the assessment of health-related quality of life, which has become commonplace in clinical research in medicine and clinical psychology. Many measures are designed for specific clinical populations but use very similar items (individual questions, for example) (Kaplan and Hays, 2022). Common examples include the Arthritis Impact Measurement Scale (Meenan et al., 1992) and the Minnesota Living with Heart Failure Questionnaire (Rector and Cohn, 1992). Despite the availability of these well-validated measures, investigators often make slight modifications and create a different measure or adaptation that is offered under a new name. Targeted measures are designed to be relevant to specific groups (e.g., people with diabetes, people with hypertension, seniors, women). There are now so many measures that systematic reviews of instruments for most major diseases have been developed, including those for heart disease (Garin et al., 2009), diabetes (El Achlab et al., 2008), and breast cancer (Montazeri, 2008). In the case of vision-related quality of life, there are so many measures that there are now systematic reviews of the systematic reviews (Assi et al., 2021). One example of progress toward harmonization of measures is provided by the Patient-Reported Outcomes Measurement Information System (PROMIS®).

Over the last half century there have been numerous efforts to develop measures that represent outcomes from the patient perspective, but these measures do not reflect a common conceptualization of health and health outcome. Most widely used among these methods are questionnaires that purport to measure health-related quality of life (HRQoL). However, because there has not been a formal ontology to specify the concepts of interest in this domain, survey instruments designed for this purpose ask different questions and address different concepts. The assumption that the constructs measured are interchangeable has resulted in confusion and disagreement in the field.

Recognizing the importance of standardization for clinical research, the National Institutes of Health supported an effort to develop harmonized measures of health outcomes. The project, which became known as PROMIS®, was launched in 2004. PROMIS® used item response theory (IRT), a method of measuring traits, attributes, or other constructs of interest in the behavioral sciences. In brief, this method is a way of drawing inferences about the construct being measured from the relationship between an individual's performance on a single question (or test item) and their performance on the whole set, which makes it possible to obtain the most information using the fewest possible questions. Thus, IRT can identify the commonality among different measurement approaches. Through its use of IRT, PROMIS® has the potential to link outcomes across studies so that evaluations can be compared directly to one another, and has been the basis for reconciling ontologies: the PROMIS® framework has been mapped to the WHO's International Classification of Functioning, Disability, and Health (Cella and Hays, 2021).

In contrast with the jingle problem, the jangle problem arises when measures that go by different names (i.e., are supposed to be measures of different constructs) correlate so highly (and may contain overlapping features) that they appear to be measuring the same construct. For example, separate self-report measures of anxiety and of depression are sometimes as highly correlated with one another as their scale reliabilities will allow, meaning that they contain no unique variance (Feldman, 1993). A similar situation occurs with clinician ratings of anxiety and depression (e.g., the Hamilton Anxiety and Depression scales; see Mountjoy and Roth, 1982).

There are more complex examples, in which a number of different, but related constructs, each with its own measures, are used by different researchers and the statistical correspondence among these measures is less than robust and varies from study to study. For example, a number of different tasks are used to measure "working memory," "executive function," and "cognitive control" (Lenartowicz et al., 2010). These measures are variably related across studies, leaving it unclear whether the tasks in question are actually measuring different classes of phenomena with variable amounts of precision or error, or whether they are measuring different features of the same class. That is, there may be a number of different features of cognitive control that are loosely associated with each other but are usefully distinguished and therefore should be measured in different ways, which have been recently referred to as "sibling constructs" (Lawson and Robins, 2021). An ontology that explicitly identifies agreed-upon definitions for these constructs would support clear conclusions drawn from disparate research into them and their features.

SUMMARY

This chapter describes a number of problems that arise, at least in part, because of the absence of a shared ontology, that is, because the knowledge structures used (even if only tacitly) lack the clarity and breadth of application that would allow them to productively influence ongoing research and clinical application. We emphasize that increased attention to the development and use of ontologies would be entirely consistent with the long-standing reliance of scientists in the behavioral domain on constructs, construct validity, and related ideas. Ontologies are not an alternative or a challenge to psychometrics, but instead complement and support psychometric analysis.

Scientists in every field develop operational definitions for the terms they use. However, doing this on a case-by-case basis, without necessarily establishing shared understanding and perhaps without attention to the relationships between the defined terms and others, has left many domains in the behavioral sciences with challenges those definitions cannot address. The development of ontologies need not constrain the work scientists do or compel them to shoe-horn their ideas into dichotomies or other relationships that are not logical. Instead, it can support scientists in addressing the use of different terms or descriptions for the same underlying entity or condition, the use of the same term for different entities or concepts (often without recognition that this is the case), and the use of different, poorly correlated measures for the same entity.

These problems in the field create difficulties in communication among scientists, difficulties in comparison of research results, and difficulties for the application and dissemination of research results in clinical and other settings. They interfere with the synthesis of knowledge across domains in the behavioral sciences. All of these difficulties reduce the impact of behavioral sciences research. Ultimately, the return on investments in the behavioral science research is limited when knowledge does not accumulate; when largely similar questions are retested as if they were different; and when findings cannot be easily synthesized or retrieved to guide research, training, policy, and service delivery.

Carefully developed ontologies are a key tool for addressing many of the challenges that constrain the behavioral sciences. We do not claim that the development of improved and more widely shared ontologies will by itself fully solve these problems, but as we describe in subsequent chapters, we are confident that thoughtfully developed ontologies in the behavioral sciences will contribute substantially to their resolution. We acknowledge that there are important issues about how uniform (as opposed to pluralistic) behavioral science ontologies should be and that there are a wide range of perspectives on issues that ontology developers confront in making decisions about how to define concepts and describe their relationships, and we consider many of these in the following chapters. However, our review suggests that thoughtful ontology development and use in the behavioral sciences has the potential to accelerate the creation, synthesis, and dissemination of behavioral science knowledge.

REFERENCES

Assi, L., Chamseddine, F., Ibrahim, P., Sabbagh, H., Rosman, L., Congdon, N., Evans, J., Ramke, J., Kuper, H., Burton, M.J., Ehrlich, J.R., and Swenor, B.K. (2021). A global assessment of eye health and quality of life: A systematic review of systematic reviews. *JAMA Ophthalmology, 139*(5), 526–541. https://doi.org/10.1001/jamaophthalmol.2021.0146

Bargh, J.A. (1994). The four horsemen of automaticity: Awareness, intention, efficiency, and control in social cognition. In R.S. Wyer, Jr. and T.K. Srull (Eds.), *Handbook of Social Cognition: Basic Processes; Applications*, 1–40. Mahwah, NJ: Lawrence Erlbaum Associates, Inc.

Barrett L.F. (2009). The future of psychology: Connecting mind to brain. *Perspectives on Psychological Science, 4*(4), 326–339. https://doi.org/10.1111/j.1745-6924.2009.01134.x

Barrett L.F. (2011). Bridging token identity theory and supervenience theory through psychological construction. *Psychological Inquiry, 22*(2), 115–127. https://doi.org/10.1080/1047840X.2011.555216

Barrett, L.F., Adolphs, R., Marsella, S., Martinez, A.M., and Pollak, S.D. (2019). Emotional expressions reconsidered: Challenges to inferring emotion from human facial movements. *Psychological Science in the Public Interest, 20*(1), 1–68. https://doi.org/10.1177/1529100619832930

Barrett, L.F., Tugade, M.M., and Engle, R.W. (2004). Individual differences in working memory capacity and dual-process theories of the mind. *Psychological Bulletin, 130*(4), 553–573. https://doi.org/10.1037/0033-2909.130.4.553

Bollen, K., Cacioppo, J.T., Kaplan, R.M., Krasnik, J.A., Olds, J.L., and Dean, H. (2015). Social, behavioral, and economic sciences perspectives on robust and reliable science. https://www.nsf.gov/sbe/AC_Materials/SBE_Robust_and_Reliable_Research_Report.pdf

Bollen, K.A., and Lennox, R. (1991). Conventional wisdom on measurement: A structural equation perspective. *Psychological Bulletin, 110*, 305–314. https://doi.org/10.1037/0033-2909.110.2.305

Bornmann, L., and Mutz, R. (2015). Growth rates of modern science: A bibliometric analysis based on the number of publications and cited references. *Journal of the Association for Information Science and Technology, 66*, 2215-2222. https://doi.org/10.1002/asi.23329

Cella, D., and Hays, R. (2021). *Ontological Issues in Patient Reported Outcomes: Conceptual Issues and Challenges Addressed by the Patient-Reported Outcomes Measurement Information System (PROMIS®)*. Commissioned paper prepared for the Committee on Accelerating Behavioral Science Through Ontology Development and Use. Available: https://nap.nationalacademies.org/resource/26464/Cella-and-Hays-comissioned-paper.pdf

Chambless, D.L., Sanderson, W.C., Shoham, V., Johnson, S.B., Pope, K.S., Crits-Christoph, P., Baker, M.J., Johnson, B., Woody, S.R., Sue, S., Beutler, L.E., Williams, D.A., and McCurry, S.M. (1998). An update on empirically validated therapies. *The Clinical Psychologist*, 49(2), 5–18. https://div12.org/sites/default/files/UpdateOnEmpiricallyValidatedTherapies.pdf

Chorpita, B.F., and Daleiden, E.L. (2009). Mapping evidence-based treatments for children and adolescents: Application of the distillation and matching model to 615 treatments from 322 randomized trials. *Journal of Consulting and Clinical Psychology*, 77(3), 566–579. https://doi.org/10.1037/a0014565

Chorpita, B.F., and Daleiden, E.L. (2014). Structuring the collaboration of science and service in pursuit of a shared vision. *Journal of Clinical Child and Adolescent Psychology*, 43(2), 323–338. https://doi.org/10.1080/15374416.2013.828297

Chorpita, B.F., Daleiden, E.L., Ebesutani, C., Young, J., Becker, K.D., Nakamura, B.J., Phillips, L., Ward, A., Lynch, R., Trent, L., Smith, R.L., Okamura, K., and Starace, N. (2011). Evidence-based treatments for children and adolescents: An updated review of indicators of efficacy and effectiveness. *Clinical Psychology: Science and Practice*, 18(2), 154–172. https://doi.org/10.1111/j.1468-2850.2011.01247.x

Chorpita, B.F., Daleiden, E.L., and Weisz, J.R. (2005). Identifying and selecting the common elements of evidence based interventions: A distillation and matching model. *Mental Health Services Research*, 7(1), 5–20. Available: https://doi.org/10.1007/s11020-005-1962-6

Chute, C. (2021). *Key Issues in the Development of the ICD and Its Effects on Medicine*. Commissioned paper prepared for the Committee on Accelerating Behavioral Science Through Ontology Development and Use. Available: https://nap.nationalacademies.org/resource/26464/Chute-commissioned-paper.pdf

Davis, R., Campbell, R., Hildon, Z., Hobbs, L., and Michie, S. (2015). Theories of behaviour and behaviour change across the social and behavioural sciences: A scoping review. *Health Psychology Review*, 9(3), 323–344. https://doi.org/10.1080/17437199.2014.941722

El Achhab, Y., Nejjari, C., Chikri, M., and Lyoussi, B. (2008). Disease-specific health-related quality of life instruments among adults diabetic: A systematic review. *Diabetes Research and Clinical Practice*, 80(2), 171–184. https://doi.org/10.1016/j.diabres.2007.12.020

Elsevier. (2020). *Scopus Content Coverage Guide*. https://www.elsevier.com/__data/assets/pdf_file/0007/69451/Scopus_ContentCoverage_Guide_WEB.pdf

Feldman L.A. (1993). Distinguishing depression and anxiety in self-report: Evidence from confirmatory factor analysis on nonclinical and clinical samples. *Journal of Consulting and Clinical Psychology*, 61(4), 631–638. https://doi.org/10.1037//0022-006x.61.4.631

Garin, O., Ferrer, M., Pont, A., Rué, M., Kotzeva, A., Wiklund, I., Van Ganse, E., and Alonso, J. (2009). Disease-specific health-related quality of life questionnaires for heart failure: A systematic review with meta-analyses. *Quality of Life Research*, 18(1), 71–85. https://doi.org/10.1007/s11136-008-9416-4

Garland, A.F., Brookman-Frazee, L., Hurlburt, M.S., Accurso, E.C., Zoffness, R.J., Haine-Schlagel, R., and Ganger, W. (2010). Mental health care for children with disruptive behavior problems: A view inside therapists' offices. *Psychiatric Services*, 61(8), 788–795. https://doi.org/10.1176/ps.2010.61.8.788

Goetsch, M.R., Tumarkin, E., Blumenthal, R.S., and Whelton, S.P. (2021). *New Guidance on Blood Pressure Management in Low-Risk Adults with Stage 1 Hypertension*. American College of Cardiology. https://www.acc.org/latest-in-cardiology/articles/2021/06/21/13/05/new-guidance-on-bp-management-in-low-risk-adults-with-stage-1-htn

Gonzalez, O., MacKinnon, D.P., and Muniz, F.B. (2021). Extrinsic convergent validity evidence to prevent jingle and jangle fallacies. *Multivariate Behavioral Research*, 56(1), 3–19. https://doi.org/10.1080/00273171.2019.1707061

Helmholtz, H. (1925). *Treatise on physiological optics* (3rd ed.) 3, J.P.C. Southall, Trans. Banta.

Hunley, K.L., Cabana, G.S., and Long, J.C. (2016). The apportionment of human diversity revisited. *American Journal of Physical Anthropology, 160*(4), 561–569. https://doi.org/10.1002/ajpa.22899

Institute of Medicine. (2003). *Unequal treatment: Confronting Racial and Ethnic Disparities in Health Care*. Washington, DC: National Academies Press. https://doi.org/10.17226/12875

Institute of Medicine. (2012). *How Far Have We Come in Reducing Health Disparities? Progress Since 2000: Workshop Summary*. Washington, DC: National Academies Press. https://doi.org/10.17226/13383

Kaplan, R.M., and Hays, R.D. (2022). Health-related quality of life measurement in public health. *Annual Review of Public Health, 10*. Advance online publication. https://doi.org/10.1146/annurev-publhealth-052120-012811

Kazdin, A.E. (2018). *Innovations in Psychosocial Interventions and Their Delivery: Leveraging Cutting-Edge Science to Improve the World's Mental Health*. Oxford, England: Oxford University Press.

Kelley, T.L. (1927). *Interpretation of Educational Measurements*. Yonkers-on-Hudson, NY: World Book Company.

Khera, R., Lu, Y., Lu, J., Saxena, A., Nasir, K., Jiang, L., and Krumholz, H.M. (2018). Impact of 2017 ACC/AHA guidelines on prevalence of hypertension and eligibility for antihypertensive treatment in United States and China: Nationally representative cross sectional study. *BMJ (Clinical Research Ed.), 362*, k2357. https://doi.org/10.1136/bmj.k2357

Kim, L., Portenoy, J.H., West, J.D., and Stovel, K.W. (2020). Scientific journals still matter in the era of academic search engines and preprint archives. *Journal of the Association for Information Science and Technology, 71*(10), 1218–1226. https://doi.org/10.1002/asi.24326

Kroenke, K., Spitzer, R.L., and Williams, J.B. (2001). The PHQ-9: Validity of a brief depression severity measure. *Journal of General Internal Medicine, 16*(9), 606–613. https://doi.org/10.1046/j.1525-1497.2001.016009606.x

Lahey, B.B. (2021). *Dimensions of Psychological Problems: Replacing Diagnostic Categories with a More Science-Based and Less Stigmatizing Alternative*. New York: Oxford University Press.

Lahey, B.B., Krueger, R.F., Rathouz, P.J., Waldman, I.D., and Zald, D.H. (2017). A hierarchical causal taxonomy of psychopathology across the life span. *Psychological Bulletin, 143*(2), 142–186. https://doi.org/10.1037/bul0000069

Larsen, K.R., and Bong, C.H. (2016). A tool for addressing construct identity in literature review and meta-analyses. *MIS Quarterly, 40*(3), 529–551; A1–A20. https://doi.org/10.25300/MISQ/2016/40.3.01

Lawson, K.M., and Robins, R.W. (2021). Sibling constructs: What are they, why do they matter, and how should you handle them? *Personality and Social Psychology, 25*(4), 344–366. https://doi.org/10.1177/10888683211047101

Lenartowicz, A., Kalar, D.J., Congdon, E., and Poldrack, R.A. (2010). Towards an ontology of cognitive control. *Topics in Cognitive Science, 2*(4), 678–692. https://doi-org.proxy.lib.duke.edu/10.1111/j.1756-8765.2010.01100.x

Lilienfeld, S.O., Sauvigné, K.C., Lynn, S.J., Cautin, R.L., Latzman, R.D., and Waldman, I.D. (2015). Fifty psychological and psychiatric terms to avoid: A list of inaccurate, misleading, misused, ambiguous, and logically confused words and phrases. *Frontiers in Psychology, 6*, 1100. https://doi.org/10.3389/fpsyg.2015.01100

Linné, C.V., and Schröder, J. (1763). *Genera Morborum: In Auditorum Usum*.

Meenan, R.F., Mason, J.H., Anderson, J.J., Guccione, A.A., and Kazis, L.E. (1992). AIMS2. The content and properties of a revised and expanded Arthritis Impact Measurement Scales Health Status Questionnaire. *Arthritis and Rheumatism, 35*(1), 1–10. https://doi.org/10.1002/art.1780350102

Mischel, W. (2008). The toothbrush problem. *APS Observer, 21*(11).

Montazeri A. (2008). Health-related quality of life in breast cancer patients: A bibliographic review of the literature from 1974 to 2007. *Journal of Experimental & Clinical Cancer Research*, 27(1), 32. https://doi.org/10.1186/1756-9966-27-32

Mountjoy, C.Q., and Roth, M. (1982). Studies in the relationship between depressive disorders and anxiety states. Part 2. Clinical items. *Journal of Affective Disorders*, 4(2), 149–161. https://doi.org/10.1016/0165-0327(82)90044-1

Murphy, G.L. (2002). *The Big Book of Concepts*. Cambridge, MA: MIT Press.

NASEM (National Academies of Sciences, Engineering, and Medicine). (2019a). *Fostering Healthy Mental, Emotional, and Behavioral Development in Children and Youth: A National Agenda*. Washington, DC: National Academies Press. https://doi.org/10.17226/25201

_____. (2019b). *Reproducibility and Replicability in Science*. Washington, DC: National Academies Press. https://doi.org/10.17226/25303

_____. (2021). *Reducing the Impact of Dementia in America: A Decadal Survey of the Behavioral and Social Sciences*. Washington, DC: National Academies Press. https://doi.org/10.17226/26175

National Research Council. 2004. *Measuring Racial Discrimination*. Washington, DC: The National Academies Press. https://doi.org/10.17226/10887

National Science Board, National Science Foundation. (2021). *Publications Output: U.S. Trends and International Comparisons. Science and Engineering Indicators 2022*. NSB-2021-4. https://ncses.nsf.gov/pubs/nsb20214

Oh, D.J., Han, J.W., Kim, T.H., Kwak, K.P., Kim, B.J., Kim, S.G., Kim, J.L., Moon, S.W., Park, J.H., Ryu, S.H., Youn, J.C., Lee, D.Y., Lee, D.W., Lee, S.B., Lee, J.J., Jhoo, J.H., and Kim, K.W. (2020). Epidemiological characteristics of subsyndromal depression in late life. *The Australian and New Zealand Journal of Psychiatry*, 54(2), 150–158. https://doi.org/10.1177/0004867419879242

Okamura, K.H., Orimoto, T.E., Nakamura, B.J., Chang, B., Chorpita, B.F., and Beidas, R.S. (2020). A history of child and adolescent treatment through a distillation lens: Looking back to move forward. *The Journal of Behavioral Health Services & Research*, 47(1), 70–85. https://doi.org/10.1007/s11414-019-09659-3

Padwal, R., Campbell, N., Schutte, A.E., Olsen, M.H., Delles, C., Etyang, A., Cruickshank, J.K., Stergiou, G., Rakotz, M.K., Wozniak, G., Jaffe, M.G., Benjamin, I., Parati, G., and Sharman, J.E. (2019). Optimizing observer performance of clinic blood pressure measurement: A position statement from the Lancet Commission on Hypertension Group. *Journal of Hypertension*, 37(9), 1737–1745. https://doi.org/10.1097/HJH.0000000000002112

Pew Research Center. (2020). *What Census Calls Us*. https://www.pewresearch.org/interactives/what-census-calls-us/

Rapaport, M.H., and Judd, L.L. (1998). Minor depressive disorder and subsyndromal depressive symptoms: Functional impairment and response to treatment. *Journal of Affective Disorders*, 48(2–3), 227–232. https://doi.org/10.1016/s0165-0327(97)00196-1

Rector, T.S., and Cohn, J.N. (1992). Assessment of patient outcome with the Minnesota Living with Heart Failure questionnaire: Reliability and validity during a randomized, double-blind, placebo-controlled trial of pimobendan. Pimobendan Multicenter Research Group. *American Heart Journal*, 124(4), 1017–1025. https://doi.org/10.1016/0002-8703(92)90986-6

Regier, D.A., Narrow, W.E., Clarke, D.E., Kraemer, H.C., Kuramoto, S.J., Kuhl, E.A., and Kupfer, D.J. (2013). DSM-5 field trials in the United States and Canada, Part II: test-retest reliability of selected categorical diagnoses. *The American Journal of Psychiatry*, 170(1), 59–70. https://doi.org/10.1176/appi.ajp.2012.12070999

Simon, H.A. (1971). Designing organizations for an information-rich world. In M. Greenberger (Ed.), *Computers, Communications, and the Public Interest*, 37–52. Baltimore, MD: Johns Hopkins University Press.

Williams, B., Mancia, G., Spiering, W., Agabiti Rosei, E., Azizi, M., Burnier, M., Clement, D. L., Coca, A., de Simone, G., Dominiczak, A., Kahan, T., Mahfoud, F., Redon, J., Ruilope, L., Zanchetti, A., Kerins, M., Kjeldsen, S.E., Kreutz, R., Laurent, S., Lip, G., McManus, R., Narkiewicz, K., Ruschitzka, F., Schmieder, R.E., Shlyakhto, E., Tsioufis, C., Aboyans, V., Desormais, I., and ESC Scientific Document Group. (2018). 2018 ESC/ESH guidelines for the management of arterial hypertension. *European Heart Journal*, *39*(33), 3021–3104. https://doi.org/10.1093/eurheartj/ehy339

3

Understanding Ontologies

Ontology is not a word used frequently in everyday discourse, perhaps even among scientists, and it can have slightly different meanings depending on the context. The committee sought to understand varying usages of the word and to identify a definition for our work. This chapter discusses the term's etymology in the context of computer and information science, since work in these fields has been the basis for one of the most widely used definitions, and it explains the prevailing definition of the term. In considering how this definition applies in behavioral sciences, the committee recognized that existing means of classifying and structuring knowledge in these fields lie on a continuum, and that varied approaches have utility for their intended purposes. We applied this idea in examining several examples relevant to the behavioral sciences. The chapter closes with the committee's conclusions about the nature of behavioral ontologies.

DEFINING *ONTOLOGY*

From the perspective of computer science, an ontology has been defined as a shared conceptualization (of the "objects, concepts, and other entities that are assumed to exist" in a particular domain) that is formally specified (Gruber, 1995, p. 908; Gruber, 1993; see also Studer et al., 1998). This definition emerged from a study by the U.S. Defense Advanced Research Projects Agency (DARPA) of how knowledge could be shared across computer systems (Neches et al., 1991). In the early 1990s, participants in this DARPA initiative argued that artificial intelligence (AI) would require the use of standard ontologies to ground content-specific agreements for the sharing and reuse of knowledge among software systems. The application of ontologies in this context was led by Gruber, whose work on an ontology-representation language known as Ontolingua demonstrated how ontologies could be encoded in a logic-based, knowledge-representation system for use by intelligent computer programs. Although earlier computer scientists working on intelligent computer systems had identified the importance of ontology engineering as a component of their work (e.g., Regoczei and Plantinga, 1987), Gruber and his colleagues clarified the role of ontologies in knowledge engineering and offered a solution to one of the identified technical limitations of shared, reusable knowledge-based systems. As a result of this work, Gruber and his colleagues helped make the notion of ontology engineering an integral part of computer science, and his definition of ontology is the most widely referenced one.

In Gruber's definition of ontology, "explicit" refers to the manner in which a developer carefully enumerates the types of concepts used and the constraints on their uses; "conceptualization" refers to an abstract view of the world consisting of the relevant concepts and the relationships among them that exist within a specific domain.[1] "Formal" refers to specifications that are machine readable and have well-defined semantics, and "shared" refers to the conceptualization being agreed on and accepted by those working in a discipline. Based on this definition, an ontology's primary purpose is to represent the entities in a domain by providing sets of machine-understandable statements and linking the descriptions and classifications of the terms and relationships among them.

Thus, in the context of computer and information science, an ontology refers to a specification of entities within a domain, which loosely parallels the philosophical definition of ontology as the science or study of existence (e.g., Stanford Encyclopedia of Philosophy[2]). According to Gruber, what "exists" is that which can be represented (Gruber, 1995). Therefore, ontologies formally enumerate the entities in some discipline, their relationships, and their definitions. More precisely, they do so by means of a declarative formalism: a knowledge representation that defines classes (or types), attributes (or properties), individuals (or specific members of a class), and relationships among class members (Gruber, 2016). This enumeration of a set of concepts within a domain is intended to help solve real-world problems by providing a vocabulary to support statements about the knowledge in that domain. Those representational terms are typically defined with both human-readable text describing what the term means (for use by people) and formal axioms that constrain the interpretation and use of the terms (for use by computers) (Gruber, 1995).

---

[1] A concept is an abstract idea that represents a class of objects or events. Concepts and relationships among them are significant components of ontologies: see Chapter 2.

[2] See https://plato.stanford.edu/entries/logic-ontology/#Ont

The committee's work was guided by Gruber's definition of ontology as a "formal, explicit specification of a shared conceptualization." This definition provides flexibility for considering the potential for various classification systems to accelerate progress in the behavioral sciences. The definition does not constrain ontologies to any particular kind of formalization, nor does it specify how widely shared a conceptualization must be to form the basis for an ontology, as long as the conceptualization is defensibly formal, explicit, and shared. In particular, as discussed below, an ontology need not be formalized in a logic such as the Web Ontology Language (OWL); see Box 3-1.

Not all ontology developers accept Gruber's definition, although it is by far the most cited, with more than 21,000 references, according to Google Scholar. In particular, some ontologists, often called ontological realists, reject the idea that ontological terms reflect any kind of conceptualization. Instead, they construe the terms of an ontology as representing entities in an objective reality (Smith and Ceusters, 2010), and they argue that the terms in an ontology correspond to universal distinctions about the world that require no cognitive interpretation. The notion of ontological realism has faced significant challenges, although it has received considerable attention within the community of scientists building biological ontologies (Merrill, 2010).

BOX 3-1
The Web Ontology Language (OWL)

The World Wide Web initially operated by presenting information using ordinary human language, but ways to code information so it could be machine processed were soon developed, and the resulting structures were the basis for what is known as the Semantic Web (Berners-Lee et al., 2001). OWL is a Semantic Web language recommended for use in ontology development by the World Wide Web Consortium. Logical languages such as OWL are used to formally represent meanings in the ontology through the definition of axioms that specify logical relationships that are useful for classifying terms in the ontology. For example, an axiom might specify that members of one class of entity are necessarily members of another class of entity that represents a superclass (e.g., that all *dogs* are *mammals*). Or it might specify that all values of some property of an entity must be members of a particular set of values (e.g., that *dogs* have a property, *does tricks*, values of which are limited to items in the set *sit, come, heel*, and other terms). OWL is the most widely used Semantic Web language for ontology development.

SOURCE: Based in part on Hastings (2021).

The Gruber definition is important for thinking rigorously about how to strengthen ontologies in the behavioral sciences. However, determining precisely which possible ontologies meet its criteria is not straightforward. Much of the discussion in this report applies not only to systems that do meet those criteria, but also to the larger set of purposefully developed resources that enumerate the essential entities in a discipline. Therefore, unless otherwise specified, in this report the word ontology refers to that larger set.

A CONTINUUM OF SEMANTIC SPECIFICATION

Ontologies are used in many different kinds of applications, including those for information integration, knowledge management, Semantic Web services, and enterprise application integration. Ontologies can be used in different ways depending on the nature of the problem at hand. For example, ontologies can be applied to improve information retrieval systems by providing a common understanding of concepts that humans and computers can both use. Ontologies can also be applied to undergird automated reasoning systems by providing formal definitions for concepts and the relationships among them (Staab and Studer, 2016).

Many authors argue that ontologies may be specified in various ways, such as lists of controlled terms, thesauri, taxonomies, and formal representations in logic, as all of these can represent formal, explicit specifications of shared conceptualizations—although with different degrees of formality. Some authors suggest that *folksonomies*—collections of terms offered as descriptors by communities of users, such as hashtag terms used to classify postings to social media—can be viewed as something close to an ontology. The committee did not, however, include folksonomies as ontologies since they are not managed systems that formally specify definitions or relationships among the terms.

Ontologies shape many aspects of human life, including media consumption, e-commerce, and the use of social media. For example, the ability to turn on Netflix and scroll through recommended movies depends in part on an ontology that the company has used to classify its content (Madrigal, 2018). Formal ontologies can be quite complex, with representation in logic that supports computer-based reasoning about the entities in the ontology. For example, the British Broadcasting Company uses a collection of publicly available ontologies to describe its content, including ontologies of journalism, politics, sports, and radio and television programs, all encoded in a logic that supports reasoning by computers.[3] These representations allow computers to perform queries such as "Find all news programs that

---

[3] See https://www.bbc.co.uk/blogs/internet/entries/78d4a720-8796-30bd-830d-648de6fc9508

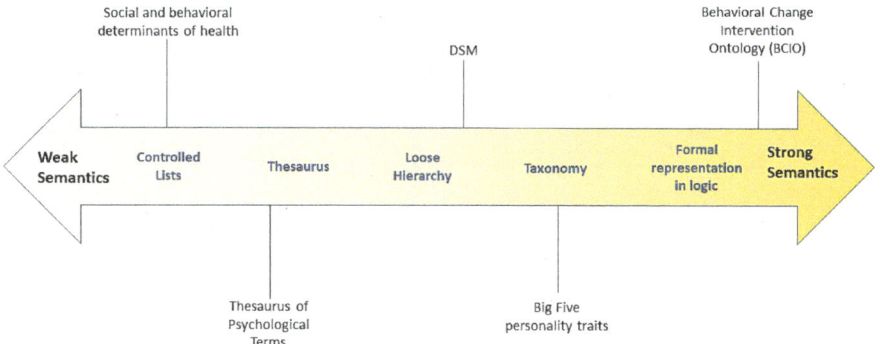

FIGURE 3-1 Continuum of representations for ontological systems, with relevant examples from the behavioral sciences.

discuss racquet sports," using the ontologies to resolve which programs are *news programs* and which sports are *racquet sports*.

As these examples suggest, ontological systems may lie on a continuum of increasing semantic complexity. That is, classification systems designed for ontological purposes (the specification of definitions and relationships) may include weak semantics (such as a simple taxonomy that specifies only class—subclass relationships) or strong semantics (such as formal representation in a logic that allows developers to specify the properties of entities and constraints on those properties).[4] Thus, we use the term *ontological systems* when referring to those that may or may not meet the definition of ontology or when that issue is relevant to the discussion.

Figure 3-1 illustrates the spectrum of semantic specification used in the context of the behavioral sciences, showing where controlled lists, thesauri, loose hierarchies, and taxonomies fall. Controlled lists, such as a list of social and behavioral determinants of health, are enumerations of specifically defined terms that help to provide consistency for users of the list. Thesauri organize terms so that the grouping reflects relationships among the terms (generally unstated): closely related terms are near one another, although exact relationships are unspecified. Taxonomies expand on thesauri by also showing hierarchical, class–subclass relationships, such as parent-child relationships, but the concepts are only enumerated: the relationships between concepts are not expressed in formal axioms. Table 3-1 provides more information about the examples shown Figure 3-1.

---

[4] The committee benefited from a workshop presentation by Deborah McGuiness in which she discussed the idea that ontologies lie on a spectrum from a simple finite list of terms to expressive ontologies that specify logical constraints and detailed relationships (see, e.g., Lassila and McGuiness, 2001).

TABLE 3-1 Examples of Ontological Systems on a Continuum

Ontology	Brief Description
Social and Behavioral Determinants of Health	A controlled list of defined terms related to behavioral, social, economic, environmental, and occupational factors. The list helps organize information and provides terminology for the causes of morbidity, mortality, and future well-being.
Thesaurus of Psychological Index Terms	A controlled list of standardized terms and definitions of psychological concepts with a loose hierarchy showing relationships to other terms. The controlled vocabulary allows for indexing, cataloging, and searching of psychological concepts.
Diagnostic and Statistical Manual of Mental Disorders (DSM)	A loose hierarchy of the behavioral phenotypic manifestation of mental disorders using a common language and standard criteria based on consensus. The DSM features descriptions of mental health conditions and use categories to offer a diagnostic tool for clinical practice and research.
Big Five Personality Traits	A suggested grouping (taxonomy) of personality traits. The grouping provides a model of the primary dimensions of individual differences in personality, and personality trait facets that form part of a primary dimension.[a]
Behavioral Change Intervention Ontology (BCIO)	A formally specified set of entities and their relationships that establishes a common language. BCIO is used to organize information in a form that enables efficient accumulation of knowledge and enables links to other knowledge systems.

NOTES: See Figure 3-1; see Appendix A for more information on the ontologies referred to in this report.
[a]The five traits are extraversion (or extroversion), agreeableness, openness, conscientiousness, and neuroticism; see Goldberg (1981).

The committee considered several other ontological systems that are familiar to behavioral scientists but did not place them on the continuum because it was not clear how to characterize them in terms of the continuum. For example, the Hierarchical Taxonomy of Psychopathology (HiTOP) is a system for enumerating the behavioral phenotypic manifestation of psychiatric problems, organized through the use of factor analytic methods (covariance between symptoms). Hierarchical relationships in HiTOP have the potential to allow for improved classification of psychopathology dimensions to facilitate research and clinical practice. Another example is the Research Domain Criteria (RDoC), a framework of brain-based systems that may be associated with psychopathology. It integrates many levels of information, from genomics to behavioral processes. We discuss these two systems further below.

The point of the continuum is to demonstrate that a variety of representation systems are used in the behavioral sciences and that these representation systems lie on a continuum of semantic specification. Considering this variety and the importance of designing classification structures to suit the needs of the researchers in a particular domain, the committee found that it was not useful to try to discern a strict cutoff below which a structure would not be considered an ontology or to classify known structures as ontologies or "non-ontologies." Instead, we highlight that the structures that exist in the behavioral sciences serve ontological purposes that are scientifically valuable.

As the Gruber definition suggests, what ontologies have in common is that they provide a structure for the enumeration of the entities in some domain: they articulate formal decisions about what is known and, to varying degrees, about the relationships among the elements of what is known, and they provide a means for sharing these enumerations across diverse approaches and methodologies (Bilder et al., 2009; Poldrack and Yarkoni, 2016; Blanch et al., 2017). It is in this sense that a range of systems may serve ontological purposes. The terms enumerated by an ontology are symbols that take on their meaning through the shared conceptualization that relates the symbols to the entities in the world to which they refer. Much of the value of ontologies comes from following a common formalization that can be adopted for many tools and computational systems. But an ontological system with strong semantics is not necessarily better than one with weaker semantics. The use of strong or weak semantics will fit a specific purpose or set of purposes, and each inevitably will reflect the relative immaturity or maturity of the domain it is designed to systematize. However, there are often times when an ontology requires strong semantics and the attendant complexity of a formal logic to address a nuanced problem. For example, the use of strong semantics may be necessary to standardize and align related measures that may otherwise be unclear or imprecise.

The choice of an ontology-representation language may also hinge on the skills of the developer. For example, ontology engineers may choose to specify their conceptualization in a logic, such as OWL, that offers a rich semantics for description of how entities in the world relate to one another in subtle ways. However, it can be hard for many novices to use OWL without making simple mistakes. Instead, an ontology engineer might use a taxonomic representation in which it is easier for novices to encode class—subclass relationships, but this option obviously constrains what the developer can say about the entities being specified. Other languages that can be used include Excel, UML,[5] object-oriented programming languages (e.g., Java), SKOS,[6] RDFS,[7] and Common Logic.[8]

---

[5] See https://www.visual-paradigm.com/guide/uml-unified-modeling-language/what-is-uml/
[6] See https://www.w3.org/TR/skos-primer/
[7] See https://arxiv.org/ftp/arxiv/papers/1401/1401.3858.pdf
[8] See https://www.w3.org/2004/12/rules-ws/slides/pathayes.pdf

When ontologies are represented in a logic such as OWL, the rich representation may make it straightforward to incorporate additional, non-ontological relations that enhance the scope of what the developer has represented. For example, one can add causal relations that allow the computer to identify how the presence of one entity may result in the presence of another, or to identify diagnostic relations that support problem solving to infer the presence of an entity based on the presence of other entities or on the properties of those entities. These complexities augment the representation from a specification of merely "what exists" to one that encodes *knowledge* about what inferences can be made if some entity is known to be present or known to have a property that takes on a particular value. Such an encoding, which goes beyond a representation of the essential elements in the domain and their basic relationships, is referred to as a knowledge base. Ontologies that are encoded in a semantically rich representation can provide the starting point for encoding full-fledged knowledge bases that support automated reasoning about the ontological entities, thereby providing a user with decision support, case analysis, or some other form of problem solving. The committee, however, focused on the representation of "what exists"—with the recognition that the creation of ontologies in the behavioral sciences would be the first step in creating a host of advanced computer systems that could reason about the knowledge bases derived from such ontologies.

EXAMPLES OF ONTOLOGICAL SYSTEMS

To gain a more detailed understanding of how ontological systems function in the behavioral sciences the committee explored several examples. We look first at an example of a formal and explicit ontology that lies on the far right of the continuum of semantic formality shown in Figure 3-1 (above). We then examine three different systems for classifying mental health problems.

A Formally Specified Ontology: The Behavioral Change Intervention Ontology

There are very few ontological systems in the behavioral sciences that have been developed using standard representation languages such as OWL. While the Behavioral Change Intervention Ontology (BCIO) is still a work in progress (as is the case with many ontologies), it provides an example of what a behavioral science ontology looks like when constructed by practitioners in the field using a standard representation approach.

The BCIO is being developed as part of the Human Behaviour-Change Project at University College London (Michie et al., 2017). The developers were responding to a problem in the study of behavior change interventions: such interventions are heterogenous in context, content, and methods of evaluation, and this heterogeneity makes it difficult to synthesize evidence, develop real-world policy, and design practical applications (Elliott et al., 2014; Michie et al., 2021). Especially concerning was the lack of common terms for such interventions, which is evident in the proliferation of theories and concepts in the relevant research (Larsen et al., 2017). For example, a multidisciplinary literature review of theories of behavior change, with strict inclusion criteria in relation to theory and behavior, identified 83 different theories with a total of 1,725 component constructs (Davis et al., 2015). The review showed that these theories tended to be overlapping and underspecified, often sharing constructs with other theories, using different names for the same constructs, measuring the same constructs using differing items, and inadequately defining constructs and relationships.

Thus, the overall aim of the Human Behaviour-Change Project has been to automate evidence searching, synthesis, and interpretation to make it easy to rapidly search for the answers to questions from clinicians, researchers, and policy makers who want to know: What works? Compared with what? How well? With what exposure? With what behaviors (for how long)? For whom? In what settings? Why? (Michie et al., 2021).

To achieve rapid retrieval of this sort, it was necessary to organize evidence on behavior change interventions ontologically, in a formal and explicit way. That is, a shared formal description of entities and relationships capturing domain knowledge was needed to support aggregation and semantic querying (i.e., finding information using not only the presence of words, but also their meaning) (Michie et al., 2021). Modeling their work on the Gene Ontology,[9] the developers of the BCIO created an ontology with a formal, rich, and explicit specification of concepts, which is why it falls on the far-right side of the continuum depicted in Figure 3-1 (above). Their ontology defines and organizes entities and the relationships among them in terms of a hierarchy using a common language that can cross disciplinary boundaries and topic domains.

The ontology for behavior change interventions was developed in accordance with the principles of the Open Biological and Biomedical Ontology (OBO) Foundry (Smith et al., 2007). The OBO Foundry represents the work of a group of investigators who promote collaboration and interoperability of ontologies in the biomedical sciences by providing a common framework for ontology development, with a commitment to the use of standards and good ontology engineering practices (Michie et al., 2021). The members of the OBO Foundry recommend the use of an upper

---

[9] See http://geneontology.org/docs/introduction-to-go-resource/; Ashburner et al. (2000); also see Appendix A.

ontology, one that models extremely general distinctions about entities in the world (e.g., whether something is a temporally limited process or whether it persists in time), captured in the Basic Formal Ontology (BFO)[10] (Arp et al., 2015; Grenon et al., 2004; Smith and Grenon, 2005).

The BFO provides a formal ontology beneath which other ontologies, such as the BCIO, are developed (Michie et al., 2021). The BFO is intended to promote clarity and interoperability among ontologies, which naturally promotes further synthesis and integration, not only within disciplines or subdisciplines, but also across them. Empirical evidence suggests that upper-level ontologies, such as the BFO, can be hard to use, however, even by developers who are well versed in their constructs (Stevens et al., 2018). The committee appreciates the stringent principles for ontology engineering advocated by the OBO Foundry, but we recognize that some of these guidelines are not uniformly accepted, and scientific ontologies that do not adhere to OBO Foundry criteria may still be valid.

The BCIO developers used a multistep, rigorous, and iterative process to build their ontology (Mitchie et al., 2021). Although the approach taken by the BCIO team was tailored to the particular challenges of creating this ontology, it is representative of ontology engineering practices commonly used in the sciences, and it provides insight into the tremendous human effort needed to develop a practical ontology of even modest scope.

The BCIO team identified 12 entities as central and common to all behavioral interventions, which are presumably familiar to intervention scientists: intervention, content, delivery, mechanism of action, exposure, reach, engagement, context, population, setting, behavior and outcome. Using these entities, further entities were defined, including such concepts as source, mode, schedule, dose, fidelity, and adherence.

The next step in the development was an expert feedback phase, during which experts were asked to rate the extent to which entity names were clear, definitions were nonoverlapping and without redundancy, relationships were suitable, and the overall structure was clear.[11] This feedback was discussed and incorporated into further refinements of definitions until consensus was reached, and the results were shared with a wider team that included systems architects and computer scientists.[12] The resulting behavioral interventions ontology has two types of behavioral change interventions, each with its own set of associated entities. The entities are related by 19 ontological relationships, such as *has part, subclass of, has attribute,*

---

[10] See https://basic-formal-ontology.org/

[11] The feedback report is available as extended data at https://osf.io/yj235/; also see West et al. (2020).

[12] The full report of this phase is available at https://github.com/HumanBehaviourChangeProject/ontologies; also see Norris et al. (2020).

has disposition, has process part, evaluates, has output, is about, difference between (Mitchie et al., 2021). Each of the entities in the final version of the ontology has a parent class that relates to concepts from external ontologies developed by other groups, including the Information Artifact Ontology (Ceusters, 2012), which provides entities of relevance for describing data and information, and the Ontology for Biomedical Investigations (OBI, Bandrowski et al., 2016).

Ontologies are not static, and they are best viewed as reflecting continuing processes of dynamic adjustment to changes in the scientific consensus, rather than as capturing immutable ideas. Thus, the final step in the construction of the BCIO ontology was the establishment of a change-management and version-tracking strategy, which is one of the OBO Foundry principles of good practice. The most general classes of BCIO have been made available in OWL and are stored in the Human Behaviour-Change Project's GitHub repository for open access. The BCIO lower-level ontology terms containing more granular concepts are reported to be under development at present. Thus, several behavioral change concepts are not yet specified in the BCIO (e.g., different subclasses of behavioral change techniques).

The developers of the BCIO hoped that a systematic approach to describing behavioral interventions and the contexts in which they have been used and studied will support researchers and clinicians in a number of ways. The BCIO, they suggest, helps structure thinking and communication about behavior change interventions. This structure can help researchers to identify knowledge gaps, to develop fruitful lines of inquiry, and to evaluate protocols. It can facilitate the synthesis of evidence and theories within and across intervention disciplines. An ontology such as the BCIO can also facilitate research that harnesses the power of artificial intelligence-based approaches such as machine learning and natural language processing for the purpose of searching databases and synthesizing, interpreting, and generating evidence and insights. Indeed, the developers suggest that the BCIO can be used as part of computer systems to evaluate the published literature and even help to generate research papers.

The BCIO illustrates the value of a formal and explicit ontology in the behavioral sciences because it provides a way to move beyond a prevalent challenge in the discipline: teams of researchers who work in silos, using data that are incompatible with data used by others in similar domains. It allows for integration of evidence when BCIO terms are shared by diverse groups of investigators to describe their data, and it makes the evidence searchable when the same ontological terms appear in both the underlying data descriptions and in the queries with which users perform their searches. Computers potentially can reason about behavioral intervention data to discover new relationships, to develop novel hypotheses, and to expose gaps in the evidence (Larsen et al., 2017). We consider these opportunities more generally in Chapters 4 and 5.

Certain challenges also emerged in the building of the BCIO. For instance, the developers reported that, given the dearth of ontologies in social and behavioral sciences, there were few existing ontologies of behavior change to draw on (Mitchie et al., 2021). It was also challenging at times for the developers to clarify subtle distinctions in the definition of entities.

There are tradeoffs in choosing the degree of "richness" in semantic expressiveness to use when developing any ontology. It might be relatively easy to define "simple" classification systems with only controlled vocabularies and loose hierarchical structures. This type of structure, however, lacks the capacity to support automated reasoning about the entities that are represented—beyond perhaps reasoning about how those entities are classified—given the lack of formal definitions and distinct relationships among the entities. While "richer" specifications allow for increased use of semantic reasoning for important tasks, such as abstraction, consistency checking, and automatic classification, the use of such approaches also requires more effort—and more skill—in defining the semantics using appropriate constraints and axioms in the ontology.

Classification Systems for Mental Health Problems

In this section we explore three influential classification systems that are frequently used in the behavioral sciences: (1) the Diagnostic and Statistical Manual of Mental Disorders (DSM), (2) the Research Domain Criteria (RDoC), and (3) the hierarchical taxonomy of psychopathology (HiTOP). While each of these is an ontological system, none has the level of formal specification that would make it compatible with representation in a logic that supports computer-based reasoning. A review of these systems highlights several of the challenges inherent in moving toward the use of more standard and more computational ontologies in the behavioral sciences.

A Categorical Classification System: The Diagnostic and Statistical Manual of Mental Disorders

The DSM has been the primary tool for classifying mental disorders since the early 1950s.[13] Its purpose is to support diagnosis and treatment of, and research about, mental disorders. The development and updating of the DSM are based on expert review carried out by workgroups, and

---

[13] See https://www.psychiatry.org/psychiatrists/practice/dsm/history-of-the-dsm for an account of the history of the classification of mental disorders in the United States (American Psychiatric Association, n.d.).

a process for establishing consensus led by the American Psychiatric Association's board of trustees. Over the years, this approach to establishing diagnostic criteria for mental disorders has generated controversy about many topics, including evolving understanding of human sexuality and the definitions of many disorders.

The DSM is a classification system for the diagnosis of psychiatric disorders: it can be used to identify whether or not individuals meet specified criteria for a disorder. That is, it treats disorders as categorically (qualitatively) distinct from one another. The DSM provides a disease code for each diagnosis in order to group sets of related disorders or manifestations of a disorder. For example, "anxiety disorders" are defined as sharing "features of excessive fear and anxiety and related behavioral disturbances" (American Psychiatric Association, 2013, p. 189). The DSM distinguishes among subtypes of anxiety in terms of the types of situations and objects that cause fear, anxiety, and avoidance behavior: for example, social phobias are distinguished from general anxiety disorder based on the idea that in the former, social situations cause anxiety, while in the latter, nonspecified stimuli cause anxiety.

All the diagnoses in the anxiety disorder class differ from diagnoses in the other classes on the basis of distinguishing characteristics of each class. For instance, the anxiety disorders class is distinguished from the class of depressive disorders based on the fact that the central defining feature of depressive disorders is the "presence of sad, empty or irritable mood, accompanied by somatic and cognitive changes that significantly affect the individual's capacity to function" (American Psychiatric Association, 2013, p. 155). These distinguishing features of classes or disorders, or disorders themselves, are viewed as pathognomonic markers of the disorder or class, such that their presence alone would render a diagnosis definitive.

The most recent version of the DSM, the DSM-5 (American Psychiatric Association, 2013), contains 22 classes or categories of disorders and other conditions that may be a focus of clinical attention: neurodevelopmental; schizophrenia spectrum; bipolar; anxiety; obsessive-compulsive-trauma- and stressor-related; dissociative; somatic; feeding/eating; elimination; sleep/wake; sexual; gender dysphoria; disruptive/impulse/conduct; substance/additive; neurocognitive; personality; paraphilic; other; and medication induced disorders. Under each of these major classes of disorders is a set of hierarchically organized disorders, each with its own code. For instance, depressive disorders include: disruptive mood dysregulation disorder, major depressive disorder, persistent depressive disorder, premenstrual dysphoric disorder, substance/medication-induced depressive disorder, depressive disorder due to another medical condition, other specified depressive disorder, and unspecified disorder.

The DSM is an ontological system because it defines the entities it enumerates, although it is not as rigorously formalized as the BCIO. For a classification system to fall on the right side of the continuum, it would have clear, named relationships among the entities in the ontology and the definitions for the entities would be expressed in a computable logic.[14] The DSM is placed to the left of the BCIO in Figure 3-1 (above) because it represents classification of mental disorders using a common language and standard criteria.

For decades, the DSM has been the primary system for the classification of mental health problems. DSM descriptions are taught in undergraduate courses in abnormal psychology, and they remain a core component of graduate training in clinical psychology, social work, and psychiatry. In addition, the DSM drives decisions about which medications or treatments patients receive and about how mental health providers are paid for their services. The DSM is the de facto structure for managing mental health conditions and arranging reimbursement for mental health care in the United States, and it is worth noting that those purposes—rather than the needs of scientists—drove the development of its categories.

Despite the DSM's usefulness for clinical and other purposes, many of its categories do not have a firm scientific base. For example, the diagnostic categories in DSM do not align with findings from clinical neuroscience or genetics (Insel et al., 2010). Furthermore, DSM classification is based on behavioral phenotypic manifestations of underlying disorder (i.e., symptoms), not on pathophysiology (the DSM-5, released in 2013, includes 265 categories based on signs and symptoms). People who meet the criteria for many DSM disorders may in fact share very few common symptoms. For example, the DSM criteria for diagnosis of major depressive disorder specifies that a patient must have five of nine specified symptoms. Thus, two people both diagnosed with the disorder may have only one symptom in common.

Another issue is that many patients meet criteria for more than one mental disorder, leading to concerns that disorders are inappropriately studied in isolation from each other. Put differently, researchers have developed their thinking about disorders, no longer regarding them as distinct categories but rather as sharing underlying dimensions that explain their covariation. The categorical emphasis still present in the DSM has led to problems, such as researchers or clinicians choosing not to enroll patients with more complex diagnoses in research trials because they wish to focus on a single diagnosis rather than the relationships among diagnoses.

---

[14] In contrast with the DSM, the Ontology of General Medical Science organizes medical diseases using such terms as bodily component, bodily feature, bodily process, bodily quantity, and the like (Ceusters and Smith, 2010). For classifications of mental disorders to follow this approach, it would be necessary to link the observed signs and symptoms to bodily (brain) processes.

For these reasons, the DSM's dominance in the field has likely hindered scientific progress. However, the DSM system is still considered the authoritative system by which mental disorders are classified in the United States and many other countries.

New methodologies in genetics, neuroimaging, and other behavioral sciences have challenged the validity of the DSM categories. The work groups in charge of the DSM-5 revisions were aware of developments in biology and neuroscience but found that the new data were not sufficiently sensitive and specific to be useful in the DSM (Cuthbert, 2014). Observers of the DSM, however, have become increasingly concerned that, although useful in a practical sense, the DSM classifications do not reflect a supportable model of mental disorders and their causes. An additional concern is with the process by which the DSM was developed, a consensus process based on the judgments of a group of primarily White, male, upper- and middle-class clinicians.

Some of the limitations of the DSM are exemplified in research on phenotypes for mental disorders. The Bipolar and Schizophrenia Network on Intermediate Phenotypes consortium collected data on cohorts of patients diagnosed with schizophrenia, schizoaffective disorder, and bipolar disorder with psychosis (Clementz et al., 2016). The research examined whether and how patients could be grouped based on their cognitive control and sensorimotor activity, regardless of diagnostic category. The data showed that the patients could be divided into three biotypes that crossed diagnostic boundaries. A similar approach was taken with patients diagnosed with a major depressive disorder (Drysdale et al., 2017). Researchers used a machine learning approach to look at biomarkers for these patients in order to determine whether there was one coherent group or whether there were subtypes within the group. The data revealed four individual biotypes: patients in each of the biotype categories responded differently to treatment. It is this kind of research that has called into question the categorical approach to diagnosing mental disorder and suggested that symptoms may be best understood (and treated) if the underlying dimensions that cause them to covary can be identified. This approach is called the dimensional approach to understanding and defining problems in mental health.

A Dimensional Classification System: Research Domain Criteria

Tying observed or self-reported signs and symptoms at the behavioral phenotypic level more closely to biological processes was the objective when the National Institute of Mental Health (NIMH) sought to develop a new system for categorizing mental disorders. Its 2008 strategic plan called for the agency to "develop, for research purposes, new ways of classifying mental disorders based on dimensions of observable behavior and neurobiological measures" (NIMH, 2008, p. 9). The resulting system, the Research Domain Criteria (RDoC), is not intended as an alternative or replacement for the DSM, but rather is a research framework that integrates many levels of information about human functioning (NIMH, n.d.-a).

The impetus for the development of RDoC was a growing awareness of the limitations of the DSM, discussed above (Cuthbert, 2014; NIMH, n.d.-a; Insel et al., 2010). The goal of RDoC was not to create a new diagnostic system that would compete with the DSM, but rather to devise alternative criteria to be used for purposes such as peer review for grant applications. This new research-focused approach would support investigators and reviewers in thinking outside the boundaries of the DSM. For example, an investigator could research underlying dimensions (e.g., the symptom anhedonia, which is a feature of more than one category) that cut across multiple DSM categories, rather than being constrained by the need to design research that aligned within DSM categories. From the perspective of NIMH, RDoC is intended to facilitate research that investigates fundamental dimensions, grounded in biology, that span multiple disorders (e.g., response to threat, attention, social processes); examines the full range of variation, from normal to abnormal; integrates genetic, neurobiological, behavioral, environmental, and self-report measures; and develops reliable and valid measures of components for basic and clinical studies (NIMH, n.d.-b). We note, however, that the assumption that fundamental dimensions are those grounded in biology implies that there is a single causal mechanism for the phenomena being accounted for. This assumption is too limiting because behavioral phenomena may be caused by a number of mechanisms (Edelman and Gally, 2001).

RDoC includes six domains (dimensions) and seven levels of analysis: see Figure 3-2. RDoC provides a framework for understanding the nature of mental health and illness in terms of varying degrees of dysfunction in general psychological/biological systems, but it does not represent the same degree of formal specification as other examples with strong semantics.

Although RDoC is not intended for use in patient care, there is some evidence that its matrix may have value in capturing clinically valuable information (McCoy et al., 2015). Moreover, RDoC's focus on systematizing normal human mental functioning and on guiding attempts to associate underlying psychological constructs of cognition and emotion with specific neural circuitry is considered an advance. However, because of its apparent grounding in psychophysiology, it is tempting to reify the RDoC dimensions as if they identify phenomena that exist in nature independent of human observation or interpretation. But the structure and elements of the RDoC matrix, like those of the DSM, were identified through a process in which

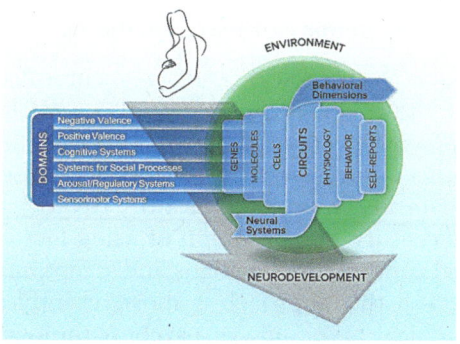

FIGURE 3-2 RDoC domains.
SOURCE: NIMH (n.d.-a).

experts identified areas on which they could reach consensus; such a process is inherently arbitrary to some extent (Ross and Margolis, 2019).

While both the DSM and RDoC systems' consensus frameworks are based on current and ongoing reviews of the empirical literature in mental health and psychophysiology, they continue to reflect concepts that originated decades ago. Those who work on the DSM rarely define new constructs, and the RDoC did not introduce any. Thus, the organizational principles of RDoC have remained largely untested, and the reproducibility of its circuit-function links is unknown—indeed there appears to be no one-to-one mapping between a dimension and a single circuit (Beam et al., 2021).

Researchers have used computational approaches to ontologies to explore how well the DSM and RDoC explain structure–function relationships and to contrast these frameworks with a data-driven one (Beam et al., 2021). The researchers applied natural language processing and machine learning techniques to the results of human neuroimaging collected over 25 years in order to redefine mental constructs in relation to brain activation data. They found that across multiple levels of domain specificity, the structure–function links (the idea that structure determines function) were better replicated in the mental constructs derived through data-driven analysis than those mapped from both the DSM and RDoC.

While several limitations in this approach were acknowledged by the authors, the use of computational approaches to neuroscience ontology demonstrated in their approach suggests the value of performing bottom-up ontological analyses. In contrast, reliance on expert-determined systems like the DSM and RDoC has the potential to introduce biases that may constrain research and limit scientific progress (Beam et al., 2021).

A Quantitative Approach: The Hierarchical Taxonomy of Psychopathology

A third approach to the classification of mental disorders uses factor analysis, which we discussed in Chapter 2 (also see Chapter 5).[15] Rather than relying on the consensus of expert committees (as with the DSM), researchers using this quantitative approach seek consensus from studies of the "natural organization of mental health" (Kotov et al., 2021; p. 86). Rooted in a nearly century-long tradition of using factor analytic methods to identify empirical constellations of signs and symptoms (e.g., Achenbach, 1966; Eysenck, 1944), this approach is most recently exemplified in the work of the hierarchical taxonomy of psychopathology (HiTOP) consortium (Kotov et al., 2021; Lahey et al., 2017).

Three assumptions guide the quantitative nosology approach exemplified by HiTOP.[16] First, mental disorders are defined as dimensions rather than categorical entities. Second, the natural organization of psychopathology can be discerned in the co-occurrence of its features: that is, using factor analytic methods, the underlying dimensions that organize psychopathology can be discovered by evaluating how signs and symptoms of psychopathology covary. Third, psychopathology can be organized hierarchically from narrow to broad dimensions so that specific psychopathology dimensions aggregate into more general factors.

The HiTOP model is premised on the idea that psychiatric signs and symptoms are captured by underlying dimensions of internalizing disorder, externalizing disorder, and thought disorder, rather than categorical diagnoses as described in the DSM (and other similar models). HiTOP aims to facilitate the search for causes and mechanisms of psychopathology by identifying coherent constructs that can be measured reliably (because the strong factorial measurement model has reliably established them) and are thus more usable and informative than traditional diagnoses. Thus, in the same way that RDoC supports use of a psychophysiological dimension (e.g., negative valence system to understand depression rather than a heterogeneous depression diagnosis), HiTOP also supports the use of a dimension, such as the dimension of negative symptoms rather than highly heterogeneous schizophrenia diagnosis (Kotov et al. 2021).

Hierarchical relationships in HiTOP allow for improved classification of psychopathology dimensions to facilitate research and clinical practice. However, HiTOP is mainly an empirical organization of psychopathology to support classification of psychiatric disorders. HiTOP, like the DSM and the RDoC, adheres to a hierarchical structure, which is an indicator that a

---

[15] See https://dictionary.apa.org/factor-analysis
[16] Nosology is the systematic classification of diseases.

classification system has specified relationships among the entities it defines. However, it should be noted that factor analysis, per se, does not result in a formal specification. While it describes the relationships between variables (through its covariance matrix), the empirical approach bypasses any kind of shared conceptualization. That is, use of factor analysis does not require shared conceptualization as an input, and the product of the factor analysis need not be anything that has a straightforward interpretation in terms of familar concepts: such interpretation involves the additional step of labeling the factors.

CONCLUSIONS

Both the DSM and RDoc are based in shared conceptualizations of phenomena, although they both lack formal specification of their content. In contrast, HiTOP is not based on any conceptualization. Rather, it offers a clear specification, not one with any formal semantics, but one derived from standard statistical inference. These three examples are each influential and demonstrate some points that arise in the development of ontological structures for the behavioral sciences.

First, in choosing a representation system—and the degree of formal specification needed—developers are choosing a language with the expressivity needed for the purpose the ontology is designed to serve. For example, OWL is a computational logic that is designed to represent rich and complex domain knowledge and that allows automated reasoning. However, it would require expertise and efforts from the developers to formally define the ontologies. A simpler taxonomy does not impose the same demands. Neither is necessarily better than the other; each is more suitable in certain circumstances.

Ontologies that incorporate relatively strong semantics support use of the ontology to create a knowledge base that goes beyond the simple enumeration of classes and taxonomic relationships.[17] The distinction between the two frameworks is important for understanding the essence of an ontology: a way of characterizing entities in the discipline, and the relationships among them. Thus, a structure that fails to formally specify terms and taxonomic relationships cannot be described as an ontological system, and one that goes distinctly beyond that function is something more complicated than an ontology.

Finally, ontologies are important tools for identifying gaps in the way researchers talk about a discipline, for developing formal definitions when they are lacking, and for testing those definitions to see whether they are useful for their intended purpose. Many of the entities about which behavioral scientists

---

[17] An ontology can incorporate logical relationships, such as causality, when they are part of the specification of terms. For example, the definition of "infectious disease" incorporates the causal relationship because the disease is defined as one caused by infection.

speak do not currently have formal definitions, and this is the problem that leads to the sorts of challenges discussed in Chapter 2. The development of an ontology is an opportunity to impose intellectual rigor on a research domain.

Based on our review of what ontologies are and how they function in the behavioral sciences, we offer three conclusions.

> **CONCLUSION 3-1:** Classification systems in the behavioral sciences lie on a continuum of semantic specification. Systems that fall along this continuum serve ontological purposes that are scientifically valuable.

> **CONCLUSION 3-2:** The classification systems that currently are widely used in the behavioral sciences do not have formal semantics, and therefore they do not readily provide opportunities to support automated reasoning and other artificial intelligence applications.

> **CONCLUSION 3-3:** While ontological systems with the most formal semantic specification offer the greatest opportunities for accelerating the behavioral sciences through the use of artificial intelligence, it is not the case that the continuum represents a hierarchy of quality. The most important characteristic of an ontological system is that its level of formal specificity fits its intended purpose.

REFERENCES

Achenbach T.M. (1966). The classification of children's psychiatric symptoms: A factor-analytic study. *Psychological Monographs*, *80*(7), 1–37. https://doi.org/10.1037/h0093906.

American Psychiatric Association (n.d.) *DSM History*. https://www.psychiatry.org/psychiatrists/practice/dsm/history-of-the-dsm

American Psychiatric Association. (2013). *Diagnostic and Statistical Manual of Mental Disorders* (5th ed.). Author.

Arp, B., Smith, B., and Spear, A. (2015). *Building Ontologies with Basic Formal Ontology*. Cambridge, MA: MIT Press.

Ashburner, M., Ball, C.A., Blake, J.A., Botstein, D., Butler, H., Cherry, J.M., Davis, A.P., Dolinski, K., Dwight, S.S., Eppig, J.T., Harris, M.A., Hill, D.P., Issel-Tarver, L., Kasarskis, A., Lewis, S., Matese, J. C., Richardson, J.E., Ringwald, M., Rubin, G.M., and Sherlock, G. (2000). Gene Ontology: Tool for the unification of biology. The Gene Ontology Consortium. *Nature Genetics*, *25*(1), 25–29. https://doi.org/10.1038/75556

Bandrowski, A., Brinkman, R., Brochhausen, M., Brush, M.H., Bug, B., Chibucos, M.C., Clancy, K., Courtot, M., Derom, D., Dumontier, M., Fan, L., Fostel, J., Fragoso, G., Gibson, F., Gonzalez-Beltran, A., Haendel, M.A., He, Y., Heiskanen, M., Hernandez-Boussard, T., Jensen, M., Lin, Y., Lister, A.L., Lord, P., Malone, J., Manduchi, E., McGee, M., Morrison, N., Overton, J.A., Parkinson, H., Peters, B., Rocca-Serra, P., Ruttenberg, A., Sansone, S.-A., Scheuermann, R.H., Schober, D., Smith, B., Soldatova, L.N., Stoeckert Jr, C.J., Taylor, C.F., Torniai, C., Turner, J.A., Vita, R., Whetze, P.L., and Zheng, J. (2016). The ontology for biomedical investigations. *PloS One*, *11*(4), e0154556. https://doi.org/10.1371/journal.pone.0154556

Beam, E., Potts, C., Poldrack, R.A., and Etkin, A. (2021). A data-driven framework for mapping domains of human neurobiology. *Nature News.* https://www.nature.com/articles/s41593-021-00948-9

Berners-Lee, T., Hendler, J., and Lassila, O. (2001). The Semantic Web. *Scientific American, 284,* 29–37. https://doi.org/10.1038/scientificamerican0501-34

Bilder, R.M., Sabb, F.W., Parker, D.S., Kalar, D., Chu, W.W., Fox, J., Freimer, N.B., and Poldrack, R.A. (2009). Cognitive ontologies for neuropsychiatric phenomics research. *Cognitive Neuropsychiatry, 14*(4-5), 419–450. https://doi.org/10.1080/13546800902787180

Blanch, A., García, R., Planes, J., Gil, R., Balada, F., Blanco, E., and Aluja, A. (2017). Ontologies about human behavior: A review of knowledge modeling systems. *European Psychologist, 22*(3), 180–197. https://doi.org/10.1027/1016-9040/a000295

Ceusters, W. (2012). An information artifact ontology perspective on data collections and associated representational artifacts. *Studies in Health Technology and Informatics, 180,* 68–72.

Ceusters, W., and Smith, B. (2010). Foundations for a realist ontology of mental disease. *Journal of Biomedical Semantics, 1*(1), 10. https://doi.org/10.1186/2041-1480-1-10

Clementz, B.A., Sweeney, J.A., Hamm, J.P., Ivleva, E.I., Ethridge, L.E., Pearlson, G.D., Keshavan, M.S., and Tamminga, C.A. (2016). Identification of distinct psychosis biotypes using brain-based biomarkers. *The American Journal of Psychiatry, 173*(4), 373–384. https://doi.org/10.1176/appi.ajp.2015.14091200

Cuthbert, B.N. (2014). The RDoC framework: Facilitating transition from ICD/DSM to dimensional approaches that integrate neuroscience and psychopathology. *World Psychiatry, 13*(1), 28–35. https://doi.org/10.1002/wps.20087

Davis, R., Campbell, R., Hildon, Z., Hobbs, L., and Michie, S. (2015). Theories of behaviour and behaviour change across the social and behavioural sciences: A scoping review. *Health Psychology Review, 9*(3), 323–344. https://doi.org/10.1080/17437199.2014.941722

Drysdale, A.T., Grosenick, L., Downar, J., Dunlop, K., Mansouri, F., Meng, Y., Fetcho, R.N., Zebley, B., Oathes, D.J., Etkin, A., Schatzberg, A.F., Sudheimer, K., Keller, J., Mayberg, H.S., Gunning, F.M., Alexopoulos, G.S., Fox, M.D., Pascual-Leone, A., Voss, H.U., Casey, B.J., Dubin, M.J. and Liston, C. (2017). Resting-state connectivity biomarkers define neurophysiological subtypes of depression. *Nature Medicine, 23*(1), 28–38. https://doi.org/10.1038/nm.4246

Edelman, G.M., and Gally, J.A. (2001). Degeneracy and complexity in biological systems. *Proceedings of the National Academy of Sciences of the United States of America, 98*(24), 13763–13768. https://doi.org/10.1073/pnas.231499798

Elliott, J.H., Turner, T., Clavisi, O., Thomas, J., Higgins, J. P., Mavergames, C., and Gruen, R.L. (2014). Living systematic reviews: An emerging opportunity to narrow the evidence-practice gap. *PLoS Medicine, 11*(2), e1001603. https://doi.org/10.1371/journal.pmed.1001603

Eysenck, H.J. (1944). Types of personality: A factorial study of seven hundred neurotics. *Journal of Mental Science, 90,* 851–861. https://doi.org/10.1192/bjp.90.381.851

Goldberg, L.R. (1981). Language and individual differences: The search for universals in personality lexicons. In L. Wheeler (Ed.), *Review of Personality and Social Psychology, 2,* 141–165. https://projects.ori.org/lrg/PDFs_papers/universals.lexicon.81.pdf.

Grenon, P., Smith, B., and Goldberg, L. (2004). Biodynamic ontology: Applying BFO in the biomedical domain. *Studies in Health Technology and Informatics, 102,* 20–38.

Gruber, T.R. (1993). A translation approach to portable ontology specifications. *Knowledge Acquisition, 5*(2), 199–220. https://doi.org/10.1006/knac.1993.1008

Gruber, T.R. (1995). Toward principles for the design of ontologies used for knowledge sharing? *International Journal of Human-Computer Studies, 43*(5-6), 907–928. https://doi.org/10.1006/ijhc.1995.1081

Gruber, T. (2016) Ontology. In L. Liu L. and M. Özsu (Eds.), *Encyclopedia of Database Systems*. Springer. https://doi.org/10.1007/978-1-4899-7993-3_1318-2

Hastings, J. (2021). *Formal Representations of Ontologies for Automation of Analyses.* Commissioned paper prepared for the Committee on Accelerating Behavioral Science Through Ontology Development and Use. Available: https://nap.nationalacademies.org/resource/26464/Hastings-comissioned-paper.pdf

Insel, T., Cuthbert, B., Garvey, M., Heinssen, R., Pine, D.S., Quinn, K., Sanislow, C., and Wang, P. (2010). Research domain criteria (RDoC): Toward a new classification framework for research on mental disorders. *The American Journal of Psychiatry, 167*(7), 748–751. https://doi.org/10.1176/appi.ajp.2010.09091379

Kotov, R. (2021). The Hierarchical Taxonomy of Psychopathology (HiTOP): A quantitative osology based on consensus of evidence. *Annual Review of Clinical Psychology, 17*, 83–108. https://doi.org/10.1146/annurev-clinpsy-081219-093304

Lahey, B.B., Krueger, R.F., Rathouz, P.J., Waldman, I.D., and Zald, D.H. (2017). A hierarchical causal taxonomy of psychopathology across the life span. *Psychological Bulletin, 143*(2), 142–186. https://doi.org/10.1037/bul0000069

Larsen, K.R., Michie, S., Hekler, E.B., Gibson, B., Spruijt-Metz, D., Ahern, D., Cole-Lewis, H., Bartlett Ellis, R.J., Hesse, B., Moser, R.P., and Yi, J. (2017). Behavior change interventions: The potential of ontologies for advancing science and practice. *Journal of Behavioral Medicine, 40*(1), 6–22. https://doi.org/10.1007/s10865-016-9768-0

Lassila, O., and McGuinnes, D. (2001). The role of frame-based representation on the Semantic Web. Linköping Electronic Articles in Computer and Information Science, Vol. 6 (2001), No. 005, Linköping University. Available: https://www.ida.liu.se/ext/epa/ej/etai/2001/018/01018-etaibody.pdf

Madrigal, A.C. (2018, December 22). How Netflix reverse-engineered Hollywood. *The Atlantic.* https://www.theatlantic.com/technology/archive/2014/01/how-netflix-reverse-engineered-hollywood/282679/

McCoy, T.H., Castro, V.M., Rosenfield, H.R., Cagan, A., Kohane, I.S., and Perlis, R.H. (2015). A clinical perspective on the relevance of research domain criteria in electronic health records. *The American Journal of Psychiatry, 172*(4), 316–320. https://doi.org/10.1176/appi.ajp.2014.14091177

Merrill, G.H. (2010). Ontological realism: Methodology or misdirection? *Applied Ontology, 5*(2), 79–108. https://doi.org/10.3233/ao-2010-0076

Michie, S., Thomas, J., Johnston, M., Aonghusa, P.M., Shawe-Taylor, J., Kelly, M.P., Deleris, L.A., Finnerty, A.N., Marques, M.M., Norris, E., O'Mara-Eves, A., and West, R. (2017). The Human Behaviour-Change Project: Harnessing the power of artificial intelligence and machine learning for evidence synthesis and interpretation. *Implementation Science, 12*(1), 121. https://doi.org/10.1186/s13012-017-0641-5

Michie, S., West, R., Finnerty, A.N., Norris, E., Wright, A.J., Marques, M.M., Johnston, M., Kelly, M.P., Thomas, J., and Hastings, J. (2021). Representation of behaviour change interventions and their evaluation: Development of the upper level of the Behaviour Change Intervention Ontology. *Wellcome Open Research, 5*, 123. https://doi.org/10.12688/wellcomeopenres.15902.2

National Institute of Mental Health (NIMH). (n.d.-a) *About RDoC.* https://www.nimh.nih.gov/research/research-funded-by-nimh/rdoc/about-rdoc

———. (n.d.-b) *Developing an RDoC Study.* https://www.nimh.nih.gov/research/research-funded-by-nimh/rdoc/developing-an-rdoc-study

———. (2008). *Strategic Plan.* https://www.hsdl.org/?view&did=755067

Neches, R., Fikes, R.E., Finin, T., Gruber, T., Patil, R., Senator, T., and Swartout, W.R. (1991). Enabling technology for knowledge sharing. *AI Magazine, 12*(3), 36. https://doi.org/10.1609/aimag.v12i3.902

Norris, E., Marques, M.M., Finnerty, A.N., Wright, A.J., West, R., Hastings, J., Williams, P., Carey, R.N., Kelly, M.P., Johnston, M., and Michie, S. (2020). Development of an Intervention Setting Ontology for behaviour change: Specifying where interventions take place. *Wellcome Open Research*, 5, 124. https://doi.org/10.12688/wellcomeopenres.15904.1

Poldrack, R., and Yarkoni, T. (2016). From brain maps to cognitive ontologies: Informatics and the search for mental structure. *Annual Review of Psychology*, 67, 587–612. https://doi.org/10.1146/annurev-psych-122414-033729

Regoczei, S., and Plantinga, E.P. (1987). Creating the domain of discourse: Ontology and inventory. *International Journal of Man-Machine Studies*, 27(3), 235–250. https://doi.org/10.1016/S0020-7373(87)80054-8

Ross, C.A., and Margolis, R.L. (2019). Research domain criteria: Strengths, weaknesses, and potential alternatives for future psychiatric research. *Molecular Neuropsychiatry*, 5(4), 218–236. https://doi.org/10.1159/000501797, 218-235

Smith, B., Ashburner, M., Rosse, C., Bard, J., Bug, W., Ceusters, W., Goldberg, L.J., Eilbeck, K., Ireland, A., Mungall, C.J., OBI Consortium, Leontis, N., Rocca-Serra, P., Ruttenberg, A., Sansone, S.A., Scheuermann, R.H., Shah, N., Whetzel, P.L., and Lewis, S. (2007). The OBO Foundry: Coordinated evolution of ontologies to support biomedical data integration. *Nature Biotechnology*, 25(11), 1251–1255. https://doi.org/10.1038/nbt1346

Smith, B., and Ceusters, W. (2010). Ontological realism: A methodology for coordinated evolution of scientific ontologies. *Applied Ontology*, 5(3-4), 139–188. https://doi.org/10.3233/ao-2010-0079

Smith, B., and Grenon, P. (2005). The cornucopia of formal-ontological relations. *Dialectica*, 58, 279–296. https://doi.org/10.1111/J.1746-8361.2004.TB00305.X

Staab, S., and Studer, R. (Eds.). (2016). *Handbook on Ontologies*. New York: Springer.

Stevens, R., Lord, P., Malone, J., and Matentzoglu, N. (2018). Measuring expert performance at manually classifying domain entities under Upper Ontology Classes. *SSRN Electronic Journal*. https://doi.org/10.2139/ssrn.3248494

Studer, R., Benjamins, V.R., and Fensel, D. (1998). Knowledge engineering: Principles and methods. *Data & Knowledge Engineering*, 25(1-2), 161–197. https://doi.org/10.1016/S0169-023X(97)00056-6

West, R., Michie, S., Shawe-Taylor, J., Thomas, J., Finnerty, A.N., Johnston, M., Aonghusa, P.M., O'Mara-Eves, A. Stokes, G., Norris, E., Marques, M., Kelly, M.P., Ganguly, D., Moore, C., Hou, Y., Bonin, F., Wright, A., Veally, C., Zink, S., and Schenk, P. (2020). Human Behaviour-Change Project. https://doi.org/10.17605/OSF.IO/UXWDB

4

How Ontologies Facilitate Science

Ontologies are essential to science because they identify and clarify the entities and concepts that people want to talk about and study, and they identify the key relationships among those concepts. Understanding of these entities may change over time but identifying shared names for phenomena is an essential basis for all scientific work—as it is for any constructive communication. Psychologists today do not investigate the *ego* and the *id* as they were defined by Sigmund Freud in 1923, but the labeling of these terms opened the door to new ways of talking about and studying psychological phenomena, and thus, despite their scientific obsolescence, their influence in moving behavioral science forward has endured.

The relationships among entities in an ontology provide essential guidance for scientific work. The ability to classify neural pathways based on the neurotransmitters present at their synapses, for example, allows scientists to relate those pathways to a variety of physiological properties and to specific drugs that may affect the behavior of those pathways. The formal specification of both the essential elements of a scientific discipline and the key relationships among them provides an inspectable, shared description of what that discipline is about. The specification offers a framework that enables its practitioners to clarify their shared world view and to communicate with one another with the clarity needed to advance scientific knowledge.

Scientific ontologies are not static. As theories are tested, revised, and ultimately replaced, the terms and relationships in ontologies need to be adapted to reflect the prevailing ways in which researchers construe their discipline. Ontologies thus do not lock in or constrain scientific thought.

Instead, they capture in formal terms and relationships what investigators currently are thinking about their field, and they clarify what a particular scientific paradigm postulates about the discipline being modeled. Perhaps just as important, ontologies help to identify weaknesses and gaps in the knowledge on which a discipline is based because they reveal omissions and inconsistencies in the research literature. Ontologies are more than just a convenient data structure; they provide the basis for both humans and machines to apprehend the structure of a scientific discipline and the salient distinctions that it makes about the world through an evolving set of standardized concepts and relationships.

Chapter 2 discusses the challenges that ontologies can address, and Chapter 3 examines what constitutes an ontology and the differences between ontologies and other knowledge resources. In this chapter we examine in more detail why ontologies are important to the behavioral sciences and the pragmatic benefits that they provide. We discuss how ontologies facilitate scientific advancement and how they aid the development of electronic knowledge bases that can assist scientists and clinicians in a range of knowledge-intensive tasks. The chapter closes with the committee's conclusions about the ways ontologies can help to advance the behavioral sciences and, indeed, all sciences.

HOW ONTOLOGIES FACILITATE SCIENTIFIC PROGRESS

The existence of an explicit ontology makes possible many functions that are important not only to scientists, but also to those who rely on the knowledge that scientists produce. In this section we briefly summarize some of the ways ontologies facilitate the progress of science, with particular emphasis on the behavioral sciences. We emphasize that a single ontology (or set of ontologies) in the behavioral sciences cannot by itself offer all these advantages: our argument is that greater reliance on ontologies across domains will cumulatively build rigor, efficiencies, and the other advantages we discuss in this report. Although the engineering of an ontology describing a scientific discipline invariably requires a great deal of work (see Chapter 5), that effort ultimately is amortized over the many uses for that ontology and the many applications that can take advantage of that shared foundation.

Clarifying the Phenomena That Are Studied

The capacity to accurately refer to behavioral phenomena is a basic pillar of the behavioral sciences, allowing researchers to be precise about what they are studying and how they are conceptualizing their domain. As mentioned above, the naming of the *id* and *ego* provided a way for psychologists to begin talking about mental phenomena that had not previously been topics of study or even topics of organized discussion. A shared ontology is particularly salient for behavioral scientists, who rely heavily on constructs to guide research, because many of the phenomena they study are challenging to organize and investigate (e.g., exploratory behavior, self-control, or executive function; see Chapter 2). As a result, these constructs are not always used or measured by different researchers in the same way. But, as discussed in Chapter 2, a shared conceptualization that specifies agreed-upon definitions of phenomena is a key to successful science. Thus, this seemingly abstract function of ontologies may be the most important of all, particularly for the behavioral sciences.

A core tension in any ontology is between the values and goals of researchers and the limitations in human capacity to perfectly apprehend and represent what is "out there" in the domain of scientific inquiry that the ontology is intended to characterize. Scientists recognize that improving their capacity to perceive, understand, and make predictions about the world is a primary goal. Thus, developers of ontologies try to capture as best they can the scientists' shared conceptualization—which, in turn, is intended to approximate what exists in the world. But ontologies also need to have pragmatic features that allow them to support the particular goals that researchers have, such as classification, communication, data integration and sharing, bibliographic retrieval, and the comparison and analysis of data. Some of the constructs of interest in the behavioral sciences—such as rationality, self-regulation, and complex emotions—may not be at all intuitive or observable, but are essential elements of the behavioral sciences that ontologies could be expected to describe. Indeed, the central role that constructs and construct validation have played throughout the history of the behavioral sciences points to the value (and ultimately, the necessity) of ontologies in facilitating progress.

Classification

Ontologies are used to sort individuals, objects, and events into different groups. For example, an ontology might classify psychiatric disorders as various types of mental illness or classify organisms as representing particular species and higher taxonomic categories. The World Health Organization's International Classification of Diseases (ICD) supports the systematic recording, analysis, interpretation, and comparison of morbidity and mortality data collected in different countries or regions and at different times (see Chapter 2 and Appendix A). The set of terms in the ICD provides a precise nomenclature for specifying diseases and a hierarchical structure for those terms that allows for the classification of diseases. For instance, the ICD declares unambiguously that COVID-19 is an infectious disease and that superficial spreading melanoma is a kind of skin neoplasm, which is a kind of cancer. These classifications are encoded directly in the ICD's hierarchy of terms.

When a scientific ontology is encoded in a description logic, such as the Web Ontology Language (OWL; see Chapter 3), other kinds of classifications can be inferred by a program that reasons about the implications of the semantic encoding assigned to the entities in the ontology. Thus, the National Cancer Institute (NCI) Thesaurus, like the ICD, may note that superficial spreading melanoma is a kind of skin neoplasm: see Box 4-1. Using OWL to define this condition may also allow a reasoning system to infer that, if this condition is necessarily a cancer of melanocytes, then superficial spreading melanoma should also be classified as a malignancy of cells that are of neural-crest origin. Such classifications may not be obvious simply by inspection, but they are provable from the logic of the representation. Ontologies thus allow developers to encode the classifications that they are aware of directly into the structure of an ontology, and to discover new classifications through the application of reasoning systems that determine the logical implications of the ways in which the entities have been defined. An ontology would allow investigators to test hypotheses derived from the logical structure of individual constructs and their relations, though as far as the committee could determine, this benefit of developing and using ontologies has yet to be widely realized in the behavioral sciences.

BOX 4-1
The NCI Thesaurus

Since 2000, the National Cancer Institute has supported a thesaurus of biomedical terms that was designed to make it easier for researchers to share data (de Coronado et al., 2009).[a] This resource is used to support translational and foundational research, clinical care, and public information. It is updated monthly and defines more than 100,000 concepts organized hierarchically that pertain to cancer and related biomedical domains.[b] The topics it covers include types of cancers, research findings, drugs and other therapies, anatomy, genes, pathways, cellular and subcellular processes, proteins, and experimental organisms (Sioutos et al., 2007). The Thesaurus is widely used in the United States and internationally and is aligned with partner entities that offer standardized definitions of terms such as the U.S. Food and Drug Administration and the Clinical Data Interchange Standards Consortium Terminology.

---

[a] Richard Moser and Lyubov Remennik, both of the National Cancer Institute, presented to the committee about the NCI Thesaurus at it Spring 2121 public workshop.
[b] See https://ncithesaurus.nci.nih.gov/ncitbrowser/

Communication

By enumerating phenomena of interest, an ontology allows people to communicate clearly and efficiently about the ideas that are represented. For scientists and researchers, a shared ontology makes it possible to accurately describe and express their constructs, theories, experiments, and methods. In particular, shared ontologies are critical for comparison of results from different experiments and observations. Suppose that one researcher reports an experiment in which praising dogs regardless of their performance resulted in less disciplined behavior, and another reports an experiment in which giving dogs food treats on a random schedule resulted in poor control. Comparison and integration of these two experiments crucially depends on whether praise and treats, or the underlying constructs of disciplined behavior and poor control, are defined in the same way. If the two researchers do not share an ontology (recognize the same kinds of objects, variables, or measures of the same parts of the world), their results are largely incommensurable.

Similarly, if the different experiments and observations are attempts to measure the same underlying latent variables (variables that are inferred, rather than observed) or constructs, then agreement is needed about the nature and measurement of those variables (i.e., agreement about that aspect of the ontology). Scientific communities and scientific progress depend on investigators being able to evaluate one another's theories and to build on one another's work, but these fundamental aspects of the scientific process cannot be achieved in the absence of shared terms and the ability to communicate in a consistent manner.

An example of a behavioral science ontology intended to facilitate communication among scientists is the Cognitive Atlas, a collaborative effort to characterize the current ideas in cognitive science and cognitive neuroscience: see Box 4-2. The Cognitive Atlas is intended to compile and systematize concepts used by experts in psychology, cognitive science, and neuroscience. Interestingly, the Atlas is explicitly designed to identify not only areas of agreement among researchers, but also areas of disagreement, such as differing definitions of concepts and constructs, differing operationalizations of those constructs, and differing interpretations of the meaning of experimental tasks and manipulations. It is intended to provide a language in which different researchers can discuss their experiments and theories in ways that other cognitive scientists can readily understand, albeit perhaps in terms that are different from those that they usually use. Thus, the development of the Atlas documents usages without needing to take a stance on philosophical differences among potential users.

Ontologies also support communication about theories, experiments, knowledge, and insights among disparate communities of practice. Consider a clinician selecting a code from the Diagnostic and Statistical Manual of

> **BOX 4-2**
> **The Cognitive Atlas**
>
> The Cognitive Atlas is an effort to systematically describe the current state of key ideas in cognitive science by establishing shared definitions and arranging them in a structured, searchable database. It was developed through a collaboration among investigators with expertise in psychology, biology, neuroscience, neurology, linguistics, and a variety of other disciplines (Poldrack et al., 2011; Miller et al., 2010).[3] It attempts to describe relationships among ideas in major categories, including mental concepts (e.g., working memory, abductive reasoning); experimental tasks (e.g., delayed memory task, two-stage decision task); disorders (e.g., Asperger syndrome); and theories (e.g., Baddeley's model of working memory). For example, many aspects of memory—including spatial working memory, auditory working memory, tactile working memory, working memory retrieval, and working memory storage—can be classified under the broader heading of working memory. The database links concepts to tasks that may measure them, implementations, relevant disorders, and other factors. This formal structured hierarchy is designed to support researchers and other users in searching databases and developing more systematic methods for organizing what is known (Hastings et al., 2014).
>
> The Cognitive Atlas is important because it demonstrates how standardized specifications for phenomena studied in a domain can be established when they did not previously exist. However, its developers acknowledge that the Atlas has not been widely used and point to several challenges. One has been the difficulty of capturing ongoing disagreements in the field about constructs and relationships; another has been identifying language that accurately represents concepts in ways that work for computational purposes. More evidence that these challenges can be overcome may be needed to convince researchers to use an ontology such as the Cognitive Atlas.

Mental Disorders (DSM) to describe a patient's mental disorder. The code enables payors to know the purpose of some clinical encounter, it enables pharmacists to know the purpose of some prescription for medication, and it enables social workers to negotiate follow-up care with other health care facilities. The shared ontology term (i.e., the code) thus provides a standard mechanism for workers from many different stakeholder groups—who have their own customs, their own jargon, their own world views—to embrace a piece of common information and to act on it accordingly. Although debates regarding the relative merits and disadvantages of the DSM are ongoing (see Chapter 3), there is no doubt that it has had a profound effect

---

[3] Cognitive Atlas developer Russell Poldrack presented to the committee at its spring 2021 workshop.

on the exchange of data throughout the clinical enterprise. Ontologies thus facilitate communication among disparate professional groups in precise terms for the very pragmatic purpose of ensuring that appropriate information is correctly transferred.

In many settings, successful communication with lay audiences is also crucial. This kind of communication is particularly complicated in the behavioral sciences because nonclinical or nonscientific audiences may have their own ideas and beliefs regarding psychological or behavioral concepts. Lay notions, such as attitudes, beliefs, desires, and emotions, often do not clearly map onto science-based ontologies, which rely on constructs that may be at a level of abstraction several steps removed from everyday language. The behavioral sciences, in particular, face the challenge of simultaneously refining and systematizing knowledge while making that knowledge accessible to a broad range of scientist and nonscientist stakeholders. Because the relationships between these everyday notions and the constructs defined in behavioral science are rarely delineated clearly, it is important that researchers use standardized terms for the constructs they are studying to eliminate (or at least reduce) the potential for misunderstanding whenever they are communicating with patients and other lay people, including policy makers. Having an ontology in place for a construct such as "attitude" will both allow researchers to maximize the scientific impact of their work (e.g., by expanding the ability to compare findings across studies) and also help to ensure that, when the emerging knowledge is shared, it is done in a manner that respects the distinctions between everyday and scientific language.

Data Integration

Shared ontologies make it possible for researchers to integrate their data with those of other scientists, pooling results and thus also making it possible to explore hypotheses with larger sample sizes and different sets of subjects. Such pooling is possible only if investigators use the same terms to describe the same phenomena or if there are clear mappings between the idiosyncratic terms that one investigator may use and the standard terms used generally in the scientific community. Unfortunately, the absence of widely shared ontologies in the behavioral sciences (see Chapter 5) has been at the root of debates among investigators that focus on differences in measurement and operationalization. Ontology development could help to move research domains toward more broadly accepted nomenclature for a topic of interest.

Ontologies are necessary for computers to manage the integration of data collected in different contexts. An example from outside the behavioral sciences illustrates the importance of this function. Years ago, computer-aided design (CAD) software existed in parallel with noncompatible software designed to support product fabrication—that is, software for computer-aided manufacturing (CAM) (Geddes, 2020).[4] These two separate technologies could not interact. Industrial designers could use CAD technology to specify new products, but their specifications could not be interpreted by CAM technology to turn their designs into actual products. CAD and CAM software referred to the same components in inconsistent ways, so integration of information across the two computer systems was simply impossible. Industrial design and industrial manufacturing could not be unified until ontologies were developed so that CAD and CAM systems could exchange information seamlessly. In the behavioral sciences, there may be a similar strong desire to integrate different data sources, such as clinical data from electronic health record systems and experimental data obtained in the laboratory, but such data integration is stymied in the absence of ontologies that can standardize the terms used in different contexts.

The practical use of ontologies by computer systems to combine data or information from multiple, heterogeneous sources has been developing rapidly and is becoming more widespread (Zhang et al, 2021). *Semantic integration* involves the use of a conceptual representation of data and their interrelationships (e.g., an ontology) to serve as a canonical resource that enables integration of data from sources that may adopt heterogeneous conventions regarding the form or naming of the data elements (Xiao and Wang, 2006). Semantic integration not only standardizes the terms used by interoperating systems and provides definitions for those terms, but also entails formal representations that store contextual information to enable both interconversion across the systems and the translation of source terms into the canonical terms needed to integrate the data in a scalable manner (Alkhamisi and Saleh, 2020). Semantic integration enables researchers to use a wide range of computational tools to more rapidly advance their scientific work.

Data Sharing

A major theme in virtually all research communities in recent years has been the importance of making primary data publicly available so that other investigators can verify experimental results and perform secondary analyses. Increasingly, the data collection that results from govern-

---

[4]For a discussion of the history of CAD and CAM, see https://www.technicalfoamservices.co.uk/blog/blog-history-of-cad-cam/

ment funding of research is viewed as a public good, and making datasets available in open data repositories is seen as an essential goal for science, equal to the goal of publishing research in journals. The critical importance of openness and sharing of scientific data has been documented in prior reports of the National Academies of Sciences, Engineering, and Medicine and elsewhere (NASEM, 2018, 2021). The goal is to create datasets that are findable, accessible, interoperable, and reusable—that is, FAIR—and the creation of FAIR data continues to receive broad support from funding agencies, professional societies, and individual researchers (Wilkinson et al., 2016). The FAIR guiding principles require that the data be annotated with metadata that describe the datasets and that are based on community-supported standards. Those standards, of course, need to include terms from appropriate ontologies.

The metadata needed to describe datasets for open science typically consist of a list of attributes–value pairs. The *attributes* often correspond to general ways in which an experiment might be described (e.g., that an experiment has subjects, interventions, and methods of data collection). The *values* provide the specific information needed to understand what was done (i.e., who or what the subjects were, exactly what the intervention was, what methods were used to collect the data). For datasets to be FAIR, the values for each of the attribute–value pairs in the metadata, when appropriate, should be terms from a designated ontology.

The datasets will not be "findable" unless ontology terms allow researchers to search the metadata of the datasets in a precise manner. The datasets will not be interoperable or reusable unless the datasets have standardized metadata that enable third parties to know what precisely was done in the experiments that generated the data. Making data FAIR requires more than putting data in an open repository: it requires ensuring that data are accompanied by rich, controlled metadata—and that requires the availability of appropriate standard, scientific ontologies.

Bibliographic Retrieval

Optimal searching of the scientific literature (and datasets) is facilitated by indexing the contents of bibliographic databases using controlled terms, which enables search engines to use those terms to find appropriate content. Use of controlled terms is important for bibliographic retrieval, as authors frequently describe their research in inconsistent ways, and there is no way for a searcher to know all the idiosyncratic ways in which researchers describe and refer to their work.

A good portion of the behavioral science literature is indexed by the National Library of Medicine, using its controlled terminology of medical subject headings through the Medline database and PubMed.[5] Although PubMed provides excellent access to medical and biological knowledge, the system is weaker in its support for experimental psychology and other behavioral sciences outside of biomedicine. Psychologists often search the PsycINFO database of the American Psychological Association (APA) for access to information concerning a broad range of journal articles, research reports, and other resources.[6] PsycINFO permits searches using (1) uncontrolled keywords (generally supplied by authors), (2) controlled index terms (derived from the APA's *Thesaurus of Psychological Index Terms*), and (3) classification codes (used by APA staff to indicate the relevant subfield(s) of psychology).[7] However, this resource, which contains over 5 million records from more than 2,200 journals, covers a very wide landscape. A recent examination noted that while the database has been regularly updated it still reflects assumptions that have become outdated, and pointed to questions about the validity of the controlled terms (Burman, 2018). As users of the database, the committee notes that because the terms are not organized hierarchically, the database does not lend itself naturally to searches that involve abstractions of index terms.

In general, formal ontologies support searches that can be more tailored to the user's needs because they allow more abstract or more granular terms related to an initial term of interest to be easily identified and used. Such ontologies may also be able to incorporate external ontologies (such as the Cognitive Atlas, RDoC, or the DSM; see Chapter 3), making it easy to identify new search terms and easing the maintenance of the search engine as the external ontologies evolve. Modern search engines increasingly rely on natural language processing (NLP) of the text of scientific documents. The availability of appropriate ontologies can enhance the capabilities of NLP: it can improve both the precision and recall of bibliographic retrieval by codifying the abstractions, specializations, and synonyms of terms that users may use to formulate a search but that may not be mentioned explicitly in the text of relevant documents or in the user's actual search request.

Comparison and Analysis of Data

Researchers can take advantage of the hierarchies inherent in an ontology to assist with data analysis and interpretation. An ontology allows researchers to categorize observations and to identify the general principles

---

[5] PubMed is a database of citations for research articles in biomedicine, currently containing more than 33 million citations; MEDLINE is a subset of that database. See https://www.ncbi.nlm.nih.gov/mesh/, https://www.medline.com/; also see https://pubmed.ncbi.nlm.nih.gov

[6] Initiated in 1927, PsycINFO provides abstracts and indexing of more than five million research articles in psychology and related fields.

[7] See https://www.apa.org/pubs/databases/training/thesaurus

> **BOX 4-3**
> **The Gene Ontology**
>
> Created in 1998 by researchers studying just three organisms (the fruit fly, the mouse, and yeast), the Gene Ontology has grown to encompass (1) a logical structure that describes biological functions, molecular pathways, and cellular locations for the biological functions, as well as relationships among classes, and (2) a body of annotations that trace evidence-based statements about links between specific genes and their biological roles. The Gene Ontology currently references more than 150,000 published papers as justification for the terms and relationships that it models. For descriptions of the Gene Ontology and examples of how the ontology is typically used, see du Plessis et al. (2011) and the Gene Ontology Consortium (2019).
>
> SOURCE: Adapted from http://geneontology.org/docs/introduction-to-go-resource/

that those points represent. In genomics, for example, the Gene Ontology is used frequently to help analyze the results of high-throughput experiments. In a method known as *enrichment analysis*, scientists analyze the results of investigations into which genes tend to be turned "on" under particular experimental conditions. The algorithm uses the Gene Ontology to identify the most abstract concept in the hierarchy of biological processes that explain all the identified genes, trying to exclude consideration of other genes that are not turned "on": see Box 4-3. Thus, from the individual observations, an algorithm can determine that, under the observed conditions, the cell is expressing genes needed for "DNA repair," "photosynthesis," or "sodium transport." The ontology's intrinsic hierarchy thus allows a problem solver to reason about myriad data and to identify, statistically, the best generalization for the individual observations. Similar methods have been applied in other areas of investigation, and they might well find a place in classifying complex datasets in the behavioral sciences (LePendu et al., 2011).

PRIMARY BENEFITS OF ONTOLOGIES

What would the behavioral sciences look like if ontologies intended for scientists, clinicians, and users of scientific research were developed to support the functions that we have discussed in this chapter? The committee highlights three primary benefits that ontologies can bring: (1) opportunities to improve care for patients, (2) infrastructure to support the mechanics of contemporary scientific research, and (3) an enhanced capacity to expand scientific knowledge. The first of these benefits is particularly relevant in the behavioral and biomedical sciences, but the other two are advantages that accrue in any scientific domain. The behavioral sciences have not yet taken full advantage of these benefits, as we discuss in Chapter 5.

Improving Patient Care

Diagnosis and treatment for one of the most common mental disorders, depression, illustrates what would be possible if the terms used by researchers and clinicians were linked more efficiently and systematically. Both scientists and clinicians would benefit greatly from greater alignment between the study of treatments and the study of the nature and causes of different mood disorders. There are excellent examples of translational, mechanism-driven research in mental health, but an agreed-upon formal ontology for mood disorders (as an example) would greatly simplify the process of designing, testing, and disseminating new and more effective treatment.

Imagine that a precise definition of an operationalized subtype of depression with a clearly articulated hypothetical cause were available and accepted by relevant stakeholders. With that ontological consensus in place, studies ranging in level of analysis—potentially from the molecular to the societal level—and covering topics from etiology to prevention, would be more easily compared and integrated. Having an articulated definition, hypothesized cause, and operationalization would help to ensure that investigators examining different aspects of the disorder were using a common language, sharing measures and the same logical structure for designing their specific studies. In turn, those advantages should lead to more rapid development and dissemination of new and more effective treatments and preventive interventions. The mental health professional mentioned in Chapter 2, who struggles to identify answers to specific questions that arise in the course of their practice, would also benefit.

Clinicians are quite familiar with selecting codes from the DSM to characterize their patients' diagnoses for purposes of record keeping and billing. However, the availability of an ontology of behavioral disorders with more formal semantics that could support the encoding of machine understandable descriptions of neurophysiology and pharmacology would allow more extensive functionality. Clinicians could access the scientific literature in a more direct way to search for studies of drugs related to their patients' underlying neurochemistry. They could easily locate the latest clinical trial results not only for subjects with their patients' diagnosis, but also for those with physiologically related disorders.

Building Infrastructure for Scientific Research

Modern science is rarely conducted in the solitary manner in which Isaac Newton did his work. Science has evolved to become a complex, collaborative activity. Funders, publishers, professional societies, and investigators themselves increasingly recognize how interdependent all scientists have become. These stakeholders see the importance of sharing scientific data and of making sure that data are available in a form that is interpretable by both people and machines. The primary product of scientific experiments is new data that are a sharable resource for other scientists. The importance of establishing that conclusions drawn from the data are justified, that procedures used to create the data are replicable, and that new discoveries buried in the data do not go undiscovered has put an increased premium on describing data in standardized ways for the benefit of the entire scientific ecosystem. Those standards invariably depend on ontologies. Team science, open science, and data reuse are the future of research, whether it is laboratory based, observational, or clinical in nature (NASEM, 2015, 2018, 2019, 2021). That future requires ontologies that frame communication between people and machines to ease the interpretation of complex datasets and to make scientific data an enduring and available resource both for the community at large and for the next generation of investigators.

By establishing shared terms for the concepts and phenomena of interest within a particular domain and a classification of those entities, ontologies make key scientific functions possible, including:

- clarification and classification of phenomena being studied;
- accurate communication among scientists and other users of scientific research;
- precise bibliographic retrieval;
- integration, comparison, and analysis of data; and
- sharing of data and reuse of data to make new discoveries.

Expanding Scientific Knowledge

Etymologically, science is the word for what is *known*. Because ontologies give names and structure to what is known about a scientific discipline, they provide a foundation for thought, hypotheses, and understanding of new discoveries. Ontologies cannot eliminate scientific uncertainty, but without them there will always be ambiguity about what is known, what can be inferred, and how new ideas build on the ideas of others. Without shared names for things, each scientist will always lack the ability to test hypotheses that build on the current scientific knowledge as a common background.

The scientific method is based in part on the assumptions through which researchers base their observations, hypotheses, and discoveries in a common understanding of what exists. Ancient astronomers named the stars. Ancient anatomists named every bone in the body. Standardizing names for the entities in the world and preserving those names to ensure lucid scientific discourse is as old as science itself. Science is impossible without a shared conceptualization, and making shared conceptualizations more explicit, more exchangeable, and more examinable will advance both science and the benefits that society derives from the scientific enterprise.

CONCLUSION

CONCLUSION 4-1: By establishing a controlled vocabulary of shared terms for the concepts and phenomena of interest within a particular domain and a classification of those entities, ontologies have three primary benefits:

- They open up opportunities to improve care and services, based on the work of investigators studying disorders who use a common language, shared measures, and the same logical structure for designing their specific studies.
- They provide an infrastructure to support the mechanics and application of contemporary scientific research, helping to ensure that conclusions drawn from the data are justified, the procedures used to create the data are replicable, and new discoveries buried in the data do not go undiscovered; framing communication between people and machines; easing the interpretation of complex datasets; and making scientific data an enduring and available resource for all.
- They create enhanced capacity to expand scientific knowledge, providing a foundation for thought, hypotheses, and understanding of new discoveries.

REFERENCES

Alkhamisi, A.O., and Saleh, M. (2020). Ontology opportunities and challenges: Discussions from semantic data integration perspectives. *2020 6th Conference on Data Science and Machine Learning Applications (CDMA)*. https://ieeexplore.ieee.org/abstract/document/9044279

Burman, J.T. (2018). Through the looking-glass: PsycINFO as an historical archive of trends in psychology. *History of Psychology*, 21(4), 302–333. https://doi.org/10.1037/hop0000082

de Coronado, S. (2009). The NCI Thesaurus quality assurance life cycle. *Journal of Biomedical Informatics*, 42(3, June), 530–539. https://doi.org/10.1016/j.jbi.2009.01.003

du Plessis, L., Skunca, N., and Dessimoz, C. (2011). The what, where, how and why of gene ontology—a primer for bioinformaticians. *Briefings in Boinformatics*, 12(6), 723–735. https://doi.org/10.1093/bib/bbr002

Geddes, D. (2020). *The History of Computer-Aided Design and Computer-Aided Manufacturing (CAD/CAM)*. https://www.technicalfoamservices.co.uk/blog/blog-history-of-cad-cam/#:~:text=Initially%20used%20by%20Douglas%20T,introduced%20in%20the%20early%201950s.&text=This%20was%20the%20first%20commercial,father%20of%20CAD%2FCAM'

Gene Ontology Consortium. (2019). The Gene Ontology Resource: 20 years and still GOing strong. *Nucleic Acids Research, 47*(D1), D330–D338. https://doi.org/10.1093/nar/gky1055

Hastings, J., Frishkoff, G.A., Smith, B., Jensen, M., Poldrack, R.A., Lomax, J., Bandrowski, A., Imam, F., Turner, J.A., and Martone, M.E. (2014). Interdisciplinary perspectives on the development, integration, and application of cognitive ontologies. *Frontiers in Neuroinformatics, 8*, 62. https://doi.org/10.3389/fninf.2014.00062

LePendu, P., Musen, M.A., and Shah, N.G. (2011). Enabling enrichment analysis with the Human Disease Ontology. *Journal of Biomedical Informatics, 44*(Suppl 1), S31–8. https://pubmed.ncbi.nlm.nih.gov/21550421/

Miller, E., Seppa, C., Kittur, A., Sabb, F., and Poldrack, R. (2010). Cognitive Atlas: Employing interaction design processes to facilitate colloboarative ontology creation. *Nature Precedings*. https://doi.org/10.1038/npre.2010.4532.1

NASEM (National Academies of Sciences, Engineering, and Medicine). (2015). *Enhancing the Effectiveness of Team Science*. Washington, DC: The National Academies Press. https://doi.org/10.17226/19007

_____. (2018). *Open Science by Design: Realizing a Vision for 21st Century Research*. Washington, DC: The National Academies Press. https://doi.org/10.17226/25116

_____. (2019). *Reproducibility and Replicability in Science*. Washington, DC: The National Academies Press. https://doi.org/10.17226/25303

_____. (2021). *Developing a Toolkit for Fostering Open Science Practices: Proceedings of a Workshop*. Washington, DC: The National Academies Press. https://doi.org/10.17226/26308

Poldrack, R.A., Kittur, A., Kalar, D., Miller, E., Seppa, C., Gil, Y., Parker, D.S., Sabb, F.W., and Bilder, R.M. (2011). The Cognitive Atlas: Toward a knowledge foundation for cognitive neuroscience. *Frontiers in Neuroinformatics, 5*, 17. https://www.frontiersin.org/articles/10.3389/fninf.2011.00017/full

Sioutos, N., de Coronado, S., Haber, M.W., Hartel, F.W., Shaiu, W-L., and Wright, L.W. (2007). NCI Thesaurus: A semantic model integrating cancer-related clinical and molecular information. *Journal of Biomedical Informatics, 40*(1, February), 30–43.

Wilkinson, M.D., Dumontier, M., Aalbersberg, J.J., Appleton, G., Axton, M., Baak, A., Blomberg, N., Boiten, J-W, da Silva Santos, L.B., Bourne, P.E., Bouwman, J., Brookes, A.J., Clark, T., Crosas, M., Dillo, I., Dumon, O., Edmunds, S., Evelo, C.T., Finkers, R., Gonzalez-Beltran, A., Gray, A.J.G., Groth, P., Goble, C., Grethe, J.S., Heringa, J., Hoen, A.C 't., Hooft, R., Kuhn, T., Kok, R., Kok, J., Lusher, S.J., Martone, M.E., Mons, A., Packer, A.L., Persson, B., Rocca-Serra, P., Roos, M., van Schaik, R., Sansone, S-A., Schultes, E., Sengstag, T., Slater, T., Strawn, G., Swertz, M.A., Thompson, M., van der Lei, J., van Mulligen, E., Velterop, J., Waagmeester, A., Wittenburg, P., Wolstencroft, K., Zhao, J., and Mons, B. (2016). The FAIR guiding principles for scientific data management and stewardship. *Scientific Data, 3*, 160018. https://doi.org/10.1038/sdata.2016.18

Xiao, J., and Wang, M. (2006). Semantic integration of enterprise information: Challenges and basic principles. In R. Mizoguchi, Z. Shi, and F. Giunchiglia, F. (Eds.), *The Semantic Web—ASWC 2006. ASWC 2006. Lecture Notes in Computer Science*, 4185. https://link.springer.com/chapter/10.1007/11836025_23

Zhang, X., Xin, J., Yates, A., and Lin, J. (2021). Bag-of-words baselines for semantic code search. *Proceedings of the 1st Workshop on Natural Language Processing for Programming (NLP4Prog 2021)*. https://aclanthology.org/2021.nlp4prog-1.10/

5

Engineering Behavioral Ontologies

What would it take to realize the benefits ontologies could bring in the behavioral sciences? To answer this question, the committee first examined what is known about the ontological systems that currently exist for the behavioral sciences. We sought to understand how they are developed and used and to develop insights about how the field could take better advantage of the possibilities that ontologies offer and the scientific or sociological impacts the existing ontological systems have had on the behavioral sciences. We also explored what it takes to engineer ontologies that bring the benefits described in Chapters 2 and 4. This chapter describes what we learned about current ontologies and about the socio-cognitive (human) processes, computer-based tools, and institutional and organizational structures through which ontologies operate and are sustained.

EXISTING BEHAVIORAL ONTOLOGIES

To review the current status of ontology design and implementation in the behavioral sciences, the committee commissioned a scoping review of the published literature on behavioral science ontologies (Falzon, 2021). The review was designed to provide an understanding of how and to what extent these ontologies have been studied; the significant findings from this body of work; and any discernable trends or patterns in the behavioral science ontologies that have been studied. The committee also hoped to gain insight into the methods by which ontologies have been created in the behavioral sciences and their strengths and limitations. This scoping review covered the general literature on ontologies, reviews that synthesized

> **BOX 5-1**
> **Scoping Review Methods**
>
> **Eligibility Criteria:** The review covered published reviews and evaluations, including book chapters in the behavioral sciences. Foreign language papers and gray literature were excluded, as were papers published before 2010.
> **Sources of Evidence:** Databases searched were Ovid Medline, Embase, PsycINFO, Web of Science, and Epistemonikos. All searches were conducted on July 6, 2021. Additional searches were conducted in PsycINFO and Web of Science to identify book chapters.
> **Charting Methods:** The charting of documents was conducted independently by a single reviewer using two pre-defined tables to chart characteristics of the publications and ontologies identified in the included publications.
> **Results:** From 6,257 screened records, 231 full text studies were examined. The final number of included publications was 50, and the number of identified ontologies was 49.
>
> SOURCE: Falzon (2021).

multiple evaluations of ontologies, evaluations of individual behavioral science ontologies, and other relevant published papers. The committee did not define "ontology" for the scoping review because we wanted to obtain a broad view that could subsequently be refined and narrowed as needed for our work.[1] The scoping review search methods are summarized in Box 5-1.

It is difficult to count the number of behavioral science ontologies that have been developed. Broadly construed, ontologies are used for a wide array of purposes in the behavioral sciences and related fields, and the uses range from large-scale efforts to characterize a broad domain to very small and targeted efforts to meet much narrower objectives. In addition, vague and varying definitions of both "the behavioral sciences" and "ontology" made it difficult for the author of the scoping review to clearly demarcate existing behavioral science ontologies.[2] This is not surprising in light of what the committee found when we examined a few of the ontological systems that are best known in the behavioral sciences to test the definition of "ontology" (see Chapter 3).[3]

Falzon developed a list of 49 behavioral science ontologies identified in literature reviews, using a combination of subject headings and free text

---

[1] The author of the scoping review cautioned that it is not definitive, noting that, although it was wide and covered multiple databases, the search terms used could have excluded relevant studies. She also noted that no formal appraisal of studies was conducted.
[2] This section is based on Falzon (2021).
[3] As noted above, Falzon's work was not restricted by our definition.

terms to represent the concept of ontologies: see Table 5-1. A comparatively small proportion of the available literature was specific to behavioral science ontologies as defined in the scoping review; a much larger body of work was about biomedical ontologies. However, many of the ontologies not classified as behavioral science do cover behavioral topics. For example, several articles included behavioral ontologies in reviews of ontologies in health care, biomedicine, and other areas (Lokker et al., 2015; Kanopka, 2015; Stancin et al., 2020; Zhu et al., 2015). Falzon grouped the ontologies into five categories: behavioral (n = 16), phenotypes (n = 6), disease and mental health conditions (n = 13), genetics (n = 4), and neuroscience (n = 10). The number of classes in each ontology ranged from 167,138 (the National Cancer Institute Thesaurus) to 41 (EmotionsOnto), though the exact number of classes was unclear or unavailable for many of the ontologies reviewed.[4]

Several publications included in the scoping review described the development of single behavioral science ontologies (Brenas et al., 2019; Gkoutos et al., 2012; Hicks et al., 2016; Jensen et al., 2013; Köhler et al., 2012; Woznowski et al., 2018). These examples are useful for reviewing and understanding how these behavioral science ontologies were conceived, created, updated, and maintained. They are also helpful for understanding the vast array of engineering processes, or lack thereof, currently used to construct a behavioral science ontology.

There were relatively few studies that looked across the landscape of ontologies in the behavioral sciences (Blanch et al., 2017; Larsen et al., 2017; Norris et al., 2019; Hastings and Schultz, 2012; Poldrack and Yarkoni, 2016). Blanch and colleagues, for example, conducted a literature search of ontologies related to human behavior using the search terms "ontology with human behavior and psychology" and found 17 that had rigorous agreed-upon definitions to represent entities and links to other resources and could represent accumulated knowledge in a way that is easily shared by researchers from varied domains (Blanch et al., 2017, p. 182). However, this and other reviews primarily provided narrative descriptions, rather than evaluations of the strengths and limitations of the ontologies.

In contrast, Norris and colleagues (2019) conducted a review focused on behavior change interventions that assessed their quality. The authors identified 15 ontologies that met their selection criteria, covering such areas as cognition, mental disease, and emotions. These ontologies were developed using methods that included expert consultation and reuse of terms from existing taxonomies, terminologies, and ontologies. However, the authors concluded that *none* of the 15 represented the "breadth and detail of human behaviour change" (Norris et al., 2019, p. 164).

---

[4]For complete reference information on the ontologies identified in the scoping review, see Falzon (2021).

TABLE 5-1 Ontologies Identified in the Surveyed Literature

Ontology	Number of Classes/Terms	Domains	Source
BEHAVIORAL			
1. Standard Animal Behavior Ontology	NA	Animal behavior	Gkoutos et al., 2015
2. Neuro Behavior Ontology	1,036	Behavioral processes and phenotypes	Norris et al., 2019
3. Health Behaviour Change Ontology	92	Behavior change and automated dialogue systems	Norris et al., 2019
4. Behaviour Change Techniques	110	Behavior change	Blanch et al., 2017
5. Persuasion Support Systems for Health Behavior Change	NA	Behavior change	Win et al., 2019
6. Ontology of Behavior Change Counseling Concepts	NA	Behavior change counseling	Bickmore et al., 2011
7. Ontology of Self-Regulation	NA	Self-regulation	Eisenberg et al., 2018
8. Cognitive Atlas	3,639	Cognitive neuroscience and mental processes	Norris et al., 2019
9. Cognitive Paradigm Ontology	400	Cognitive and behavioral experiments	Norris et al., 2019
10. EmotionsOnto	41	Emotions	Norris et al., 2019
11. Emotion Ontology	902	Emotions	Norris et al., 2019
12. Exposure Ontology	148	Exposure science, genomics and toxicology	Norris et al., 2019
13. Lifestyle Ontology	NA	Life-style concepts	Benmimoune et al., 2015
14. OntoPsychia	1,450	Social and environmental determinants for psychiatry	Blanch et al., 2017
15. Semantic Mining of Activity, Social and Health Data	87	Health care data and sustained weight loss	Norris et al., 2019
16. Mental Functioning Ontology	692	Mental functioning and mental processes	Norris et al., 2019
PHENOTYPES			
17. Autism Spectrum Disorder Phenotype	284	Autism spectrum disorder phenotype	Amith et al., 2018

TABLE 5-1 Continued

Ontology	Number of Classes/Terms	Domains	Source
18. Human Phenotype Ontology	13,000	Phenotypes	Gkoutos et al., 2015
19. Mammalian Phenotype Ontology	1,528	Phenotypes	Köhler et al., 2012
20. Phenotype and Exposures	533	Phenotypes	Blanch et al., 2017
21. Measurement Method Ontology	701	Methods used to make qualitative and quantitative clinical and phenotype measurement	Yu and Shen, 2016
22. Phenotype and Trait Ontology	5,607	Biodiversity and ecology, plant phenotypes and traits	Köhler et al., 2012
DISEASE AND MENTAL HEALTH CONDITIONS			
23. Disease Ontology	NA	Disease	Gkoutos et al., 2015
24. Human Disease Ontology	12,498	Disease	Norris et al., 2019
25. Symptom Ontology	942	Symptom and disease	Norris et al., 2019
26. Alzheimer's Disease Ontology	1565	Alzheimer's disease	Amith et al., 2018
27. Bilingual Ontology of Alzheimer's Disease and Related Diseases	5,899	Alzheimer's disease	Amith et al., 2018
28. National Cancer Institute Thesaurus	167,138	Cancer	Blaum et al., 2013
29. Advancing Clinico-genomic Trials on Cancer – Open Grid Services for Improving Medical Knowledge Discovery (ACGT) Master Ontology	NA	Cancer research and management	Brochhausen et al., 2011
30. Adolescents' Depression Ontology	419	Depression	Jung et al., 2016
31. Epidemiology Ontology	191	Epidemiology	Norris et al., 2019
32. Epilepsy and Seizure Ontology	NA	Epilepsy and seizure	Yu and Shen, 2016
33. Mental Disease Ontology	1,127	Mental disease	Norris et al., 2019

continued

TABLE 5-1 Continued

Ontology	Number of Classes/Terms	Domains	Source
34. Haghighi-Koeda Mood Disorder Ontology	NA	Mood disorder	Yu and Shen, 2016
35. Neurological Disease Ontology	700	Neurological disease and phenotypes	Jensen et al., 2013
GENETICS			
36. Gene Ontology	43,850	Genetics	Blaum et al., 2013
37. Micro Array Gene Expression Data Ontology	NA	Microarray data and experiments	Wu and Yamaguchi, 2014
38. Ontology for Genetic Susceptibility	127	Genomic and proteomic health	Amith et al., 2018
39. Pharmacogenetics Relationships Ontology	229	Pharmacogenetics	Amith et al., 2018
NEUROSCIENCE			
40. Biomedical Informatics Research Network Project Lexicon	3,580	Neurons and neuronal systems	Hastings and Schultz, 2012
41. Chemical Entities of Biological Interest	165,081	Neurotransmitters	Hastings and Schultz, 2012
42. Consortium for Neuropsychiatric Phenomics	NA	Neuropsychiatric disorders	Blanch et al., 2017
43. OntoNeuroLOG	1016	Neuroimaging	Blanch et al., 2017
44. Neural Electromagnetic Ontology	1,851	Biological process	Blanch et al., 2017
45. Neuroinformatics Network	NA	Neuroinformatics	Gkoutos et al., 2015
46. Neuroimaging Data Model	161	Neuroimaging	Blanch et al., 2017
47. Neuropsychological Testing Ontology	NA	Neuropsychological testing	Gkoutos et al., 2015
48. NeuroLex	NA	Neurons and neuronal systems	Hastings and Schultz, 2012
49. Neuroscience Information Framework Ontology	124,337	Neuroscience	Blanch et al., 2017

NOTE: NA means not available.
SOURCE: Falzon (2021, Table 1).

Poldrack and Yarkoni (2016) describe the contributions that formal cognitive ontologies could make to the clarification, refinement, and testing of theories about the delineation of how brain systems relate to mental function. They argue that ontologies could potentially play a valuable role in the behavioral sciences. Similarly, Larsen and colleagues (2017) review the problems an ontology can help to solve and use ongoing work on ontologies related to behavior change to discuss key steps in ontology development.

Several other studies identified by the scoping review discuss best practices and lessons learned. As noted above, Larsen and colleagues (2017) provide multiple rationales for the creation of ontologies in the behavioral sciences and a guideline for how they should be created and could be used to advance the field of behavioral medicine. Norris and colleagues (2021) argue that behavioral science ontology development should involve expert stakeholders. Several other studies provided more formal evaluations of existing ontologies.

As mentioned above, six studies identified in the scoping review were evaluations of a single behavioral science ontology (Brenas et al., 2019; Gkoutos et al., 2012; Hicks et al., 2016; Jensen et al., 2013; Köhler et al., 2012; Woznowski et al., 2018). Other studies not exclusive to the behavioral sciences suggested criteria for evaluation: tools, methods, and software and metrics (see, e.g., Amith et al., 2018; Yao et al., 2011; Franco et al., 2020). The scoping review (Falzon, 2021) did not identify any metanalyses of evaluation approaches, but did identify various criteria in the literature for evaluating the methods and quality of an ontology (broadly understood):

- uses existing taxonomies;
- uses existing terminologies;
- uses existing ontologies;
- user feedback;
- data driven;
- unique uniform resource identifiers;
- clear definitions;
- clear structure;
- logically consistent;
- evaluated;
- maintained;
- domain coverage;
- task orientation;
- computational efficiency; and
- maps to existing technologies.

These characteristics suggest the properties that are identified as important in the available studies (see below for further discussion of evaluation; also see Chapter 4).

The scoping review also revealed a wide array of applications for existing ontologies in research, clinical settings, and education. These applications and functions closely track many of the elements identified in the committee's use case survey (see Chapter 2):[5]

- support collaborative and multidisciplinary research;
- support efficient knowledge accumulation;
- organization and structuring of evidence;
- enhanced evidence synthesis;
- automation of meta-analysis;
- analysis of raw data and integrating of findings across domains and subject areas;
- refine diagnostic categories;
- interrogate clinical information systems;
- translate research results across disciplines;
- compile lists of behavior change techniques, implementation strategies, and interventions;
- annotation (e.g., automated annotation of radiology images);
- terminology mapping (e.g., mapping terminology to phenotypic clinical data to advance knowledge of genetic diseases);
- use of natural language processing to code text from clinical documents;
- query enhancement (use of search terms to recognize context and provide synonyms and additional terms to enhance the query);
- clarify, refine, and test theories;
- code randomized clinical trials (e.g., in neurosurgery);
- develop educational software;
- personalize and recommend content;
- design curricula; and
- assess the learning process.

The authors of many of the studies discussed in the scoping review offer strong reasons why progress in ontology development and use would be a boost in the behavioral sciences (e.g., Poldrack and Yarkoni, 2016; Hastings and Schultz, 2012; Blanch et al., 2017; Larsen et al., 2017; Norris et al., 2019). The literature also offers a wealth of recommendations, many very detailed, for developing individual ontologies for targeted purposes, as well as varying guidelines for evaluating existing ones.

---

[5] See Falzon (2021, p. 13–14) for specific citations.

More elusive is a solid picture of how many models in current use can be accurately classified as ontologies, rather than sets of concepts that have not been formally specified. The scoping review did not locate any systematic documentation of existing ontologies (broadly understood), and we note that carrying out such a systematic survey would be challenging. As the continuum presented in Chapter 3 demonstrates, ontological systems vary in their degree of formal specification. We noted there that whether a given system meets the definition of ontology is less important than whether it is designed to suit the purpose for which researchers need it. The fact that the Behaviour Change Intervention Ontology (BCIO) did not turn up in the scoping review, despite being a relatively well known system that provides a high degree of formal specification, illustrates the challenge: in response to a query, the author of the scoping review noted that, although the BCIO is mentioned in two of the reviews, the literature on the project itself did not match the search terms used. While other examples could possibly have been missed in the scoping review for similar reasons, this example illustrates that it is probably more useful to apply available resources in support of researchers who wish to pursue ontological rigor than to more systematically survey existing efforts, which are both evolving and idiosyncratic.

It is also difficult to develop a picture of the extent to which existing ontological systems are currently contributing to progress in the behavioral sciences or the gaps and barriers to their development in the behavioral sciences. It was clear from both the scoping review and the committee's close look at a number of examples that many individuals have worked tirelessly on ontological efforts that apply in some way to the behavioral sciences. It was also clear that efforts to date in the behavioral sciences have not yet by any means taken full advantage of the potential benefits of ontology development. While a systematic survey of existing behavioral ontologies was well beyond the scope of this study, we did identify some trends across the ontological systems we examined, including key examples from biomedicine.

There are comparatively few ontological systems in the behavioral sciences that are widely known and used, and those that exist have had limited impact. For example, despite the efforts that have gone into their development, the Behaviour Change Intervention Ontology and the Cognitive Atlas have received relatively few citations in the academic literature in comparison with ontologies in other fields. Many ontological efforts have been isolated, and it appears that adoption and use of many existing ontological systems has been constrained. Moreover, the developers of these systems in behavioral domains appear to operate largely on their own in identifying or developing the models and practices that might best suit their needs. Few of the examples we saw took advantage of ontology best practices or computational tools or advances. None was sponsored by a central professional organization. Most appeared to have been built because of the specific interest of their creator, rather than in response to needs identified by the field. None had a sustained source of funding, and the committee heard from a variety of experts that it is difficult to sustain ontology development efforts. (We review the question of resources and support more fully in Chapter 6.)

THE ONTOLOGY ENGINEERING PROCESS: SOCIO-COGNITIVE PRACTICES

Humans must make key decisions about the terms and relationships to be covered in an ontology. Thus, socio-cognitive (social and intellectual) practices (elements or functions) are one of the two basic components of the process of engineering ontologies. Ontology engineering is a creative and inventive process that requires substantial intellectual and social effort, realized through socio-cognitive practices. The work of ontology creation, editing, dissemination, debugging, and understanding all require such practices, and the impacts of these practices at all stages of the ontology life-cycle cannot be fully captured solely by the formal specification at one moment or even over time. This section identifies some of the key socio-cognitive elements that are involved in ontology engineering, including the knowledge humans have, their activities, and their interactions with technology (social interactions, cognitive strategies, language, and patterns of communication). Best practices for some of these have been identified and are likely to be useful in the specific context of the behavioral sciences, though there are as yet few examples of their use in this context.

Creation

The creation of an ontology almost always requires the translation of complex, potentially ambiguous concepts into a formal specification. A first step in ontology creation is the identification of the key notions, as well as key features or attributes of those notions, that will be included in the ontology. Meta-analyses and critical literature reviews can provide valuable insights about which concepts are most important in a particular domain, though they will rarely be sufficient to uniquely determine what should be included in the formal specification. Almost always, experts are needed to determine how the key concepts and features should be formally represented.

A common emphasis on and approach to creating ontologies in the behavioral sciences would likely reduce the chances of unhelpful pluralism. There have been some efforts to develop *design patterns* to support ontology creation—relatively formal specifications of characteristic patterns (Blomqvist and Sandkuhl, 2005; Hitzler et al., 2016). As a simple example, an ontology design pattern for "inheritance" would provide a template for "inheritance" relational structures within the ontology, regardless of whether one means inheritance in genes, in culture, in software, or in some other domain. Design patterns have proven quite useful in other disciplines involving context-specific, complex concepts and ideas (e.g., architecture, software engineering, human-computer interaction); thus, they are a potentially promising avenue even if there is currently little empirical evidence about their utility in the behavioral sciences.

Ontologies can be used for multiple purposes (see Chapters 3 and 4). The value of a particular ontology may depend partly on intended uses, and so those uses should be clearly articulated in the creation stage of an ontology. Ontology creation should thus also involve identification of the stakeholders who may be affected by the ontology, the goals and knowledge bases that will depend on it, and key use cases (see Chapter 2). Developers might sometimes identify the goals simply by reflecting on their own needs and practices. More commonly, however, they will need to perform cognitive task analyses of the stakeholders' relevant scientific practices and papers to determine when an ontology might be useful and how it might be used (Crandall et al., 2006; Hollnagel, 2003). Proper design and use of an ontology requires an understanding of the contexts in which it will be used, whether from personal introspection or structured investigation.

Socio-cognitive practices are also important once an ontology has been created or proposed. The dissemination of an ontology involves not only transmission of the formal specification, but also instruction about ways to use it. The mappings from objects in the world to elements in the ontology can be very complex and sensitive to context, particularly in the behavioral sciences. The formal specification alone is insufficient to determine how to use an ontology. As result, unless there is already very substantial agreement in the scientific community, instruction and training will typically be needed to ensure that people use the ontology properly and not merely hear about it.

Debugging an ontology requires an understanding of what should—and equally importantly, should *not*—be included in the ontology (i.e., what is important in the domain). The basic idea of debugging an ontology is to determine the logical implications of what is in the current ontology, perhaps augmented with a minimal knowledge base, and then either include the ontology elements that support those implications, if the implications are correct, or revise the ontology if they are incorrect. This stage thus presupposes that there are some basic facts about a domain that are almost universally accepted in the scientific community. There will almost certainly not be an explicit list of such constraints on an ontology; rather, the widely accepted facts or statements will need to be determined using socio-cognitive practices of analysis and collaboration, just as such practices are needed for identification of key features and concepts for the original ontology creation. This is a critical step, but also one for which best practices have not necessarily been developed. Once some statements have been identified, formal computational tools can be used to automate aspects of debugging (see below). But the relevant constraints for debugging will typically emerge only after careful investigation.

Change and Evolution

Socio-cognitive practices also play a key role in ontology change and evolution. Because ontologies are formal specifications, it is easy to mistake them for relatively static structures. After all, they are expressed, used, and evaluated at fixed moments in time. But ontologies are dynamic: they evolve and change significantly and sometimes rapidly in response to scientific developments and other factors. Moreover, some ontologies will need to evolve in response to a complicated, open world, while others may need to be responsive to pressures from the more "closed" worlds of, say, billing practices. In almost every case, socio-cognitive factors and processes play key roles. We do not attempt to provide an exhaustive taxonomy of ontology change, but instead provide several illustrative examples.

First, ontology change could be required when scientists learn more about the world, including how the world itself might have changed or be changing. There are many instances in which a scientific community recognized that its current shared understanding was faulty or incomplete, and so any shared ontology had to be adapted in light of this new information. For example, the spread of novel diseases (e.g., COVID-19, Zika, etc.) has required additions to existing ontologies for disease classification. These ontology changes frequently involve significant communication and collaboration in the scientific community.

A second type of ontology evolution arises when scientific goals and needs shift, perhaps in response to technological advances. For example, there can be "function creep" of an ontology as it is gradually used for purposes other than the original goals. This creep can produce gradual changes in the ontology to support the new goals, though often without explicit acknowledgment that anything is changing. Ontologies can thus end up serving very different use cases than their designers originally intended.

A third kind of ontology change is prompted by the desire to harmonize or integrate different ontologies, including the desire to bridge ontologies at different levels. This particular driver of ontology change often occurs at the same time as one of the others, such as when the development of new measurement methods enables scientists to start to bridge between different domains or systems. In practice, such integrations almost always require changes to one or more ontologies, or perhaps the creation of a new ontology to replace or even to compete with the previous ones.

This dynamic can be readily seen in proposals to change aspects of mental health ontologies to better ground them in biological bases: that is, there are efforts to change an ontology so that it better integrates with another one. More generally, there are clear challenges to harmonization of medical ontologies with (potential) behavioral ones, though doing so would be valuable. Such integrations require the careful development of mappings between elements of one ontology with those of another, ideally paired with specification of bridge principles to enable expression of one ontology in the formal language of the other. At the least, there must be clear understanding of how elements of one ontology impose constraints on the possibilities for the other. Moreover, these translation efforts can often be guided by novel empirical data collected during the course of the integration process.

Ontology change can also be driven by factors that are external to scientific communities, such as cultural changes in conceptualizations. Social expectations, needs, values, and concepts can all change over time, and so there can be pressure—social, political, psychological—to adjust a scientific ontology so that it is more consistent with those social factors. For example, changes in cultural perceptions of homosexuality, pregnancy, and hysteria each played a role in subsequent changes to disease classifications. The committee does not take a position about whether or when scientific ontologies ought to respond to this type of reason for ontology change; rather, we simply note that some ontology change seems to happen because of social and cultural evolution.

All of these instances of ontology change involve socio-cognitive practices and factors. For example, an ontology might change through open discussion and debate in the relevant scientific communities, as researchers and clinicians frequently work to revise and refine their shared ontologies (and understandings, more generally). There is little consensus about best practices for scientific communities to develop shared languages and understandings. Alternately, one could crowdsource observations about shortcomings of an ontology to help ensure that diverse perspectives are being included, particularly for ontologies with significant social impact. Or methods to integrate or harmonize distinct scientific theories can provide mechanisms to reconcile or adjust different ontologies, at least if the theories are sufficiently well specified that the core ontology is clear. It is important to note that, although ontology change depends on various socio-cognitive interactions and practices, it is not merely a matter of chance or power. Rather, there are structured and semi-structured mechanisms for intelligently updating or revising an ontology.

The Role of Institutions

Organizations and institutions can play critical roles in the creation, editing, dissemination, adoption, and revision of ontologies. In particular, institutions—including universities, research funders, journals, and conferences—can create, perhaps implicitly, incentives to use or not use ontologies in various ways. A non-ontology example—regarding the growing recognition of the importance of open data—illustrates the importance of the role of institutions. There were significant changes in open data and data-sharing practices once funding agencies started to require that funded projects share their data (or provide clear, good arguments why data sharing was not appropriate or feasible). Similarly, many journals began requiring that data be made publicly available (or provide a justification as to why not) as a condition of publication. These and other institutional changes have had a significant impact on the forms and frequency of data sharing across multiple scientific disciplines. Similarly, advances in ontology creation, dissemination, and use in the behavioral sciences may require institutional changes, including incentives of various types.

The committee could not identify any existing institutional structures or incentives that directly promote the use of shared ontologies in the behavioral sciences. Practicing clinical psychology and psychiatry in an academic setting clearly requires the use of ontologies. Scholarship increasingly requires data sharing, which also requires ontologies (see Chapter 4). These are indirect incentives, but, for example, to the best of our knowledge, no university requires or prioritizes ontology (re)use when considering promotion and tenure decisions. Some journals require the selection of keywords from a fixed list, but they do not require any accompanying formal specification. Journals may also require that the data described in scientific papers be made publicly available, which, as noted above, explicitly requires ontologies, but this is rarely explicit in journal policies. No U.S. government funding agencies in the behavioral sciences currently require the use of ontologies in grant proposals or other contracts. The same appears to be true for a range of different institutions and structures that support research in the behavioral sciences. We also note that many journals, conferences, and promotion committees favor the use of novel theories and theoretical concepts, yet they do not prioritize the use of formal specifications.

Significantly, the committee also could not identify any significant *disincentives* to the use of ontologies in the behavioral sciences beyond those already noted (e.g., the "toothbrush problem") or those that apply in any complex, collaborative setting (e.g., the difficulties of team science). Institutions do not seem to be actively blocking the creation, adoption, or use of ontologies, even if they are generally not providing positive support or inducements. Yet, given that ontology creation, adoption, and use all involve some costs to researchers, it may not be surprising that systematic, shared ontology use in the behavioral sciences has been relatively rare despite the ways ontologies can help with persistent scientific challenges.

Evaluation

Determining whether an ontology is—and remains—useful for the purposes it was designed for is a key to its ongoing viability. Two important components of such an evaluation are verification and validation. Verification is the assessment of whether the ontology was built correctly, that is, whether the specification has utility for its intended purpose. Validation is determining whether the ontology correctly models the domain or real-world application for which it was intended. Essentially, verification addresses the intrinsic aspects of the ontology; validation addresses the extrinsic aspects of the ontology. Metrics such as completeness, accuracy, consistency, computational efficiency, and clarity, among others, are used in this process, and the ontologies literature includes many guides to evaluation, including many highly technical ones (see, e.g., Amith et al., 2018; Obrst et al., 2007; Rensselaer Polytechnic Institute, 2013). We also note that Gruber (1995; also see Chapter 3) identified criteria that can be used to guide the development of ontologies to ensure that the ontologies are well suited for reuse for different purposes and across applications: see Box 5-2. The Open Biological and Biomedical Ontology (OBO) Foundry has also provided a set of principles to guide those who commit to its approach (Jackson et al., 2021). These design criteria are all defined with knowledge sharing and interoperability among users of the shared conceptualization as the main purpose.

BOX 5-2
Gruber's Criteria for Developing Ontologies Intended for Reuse

1. Clarity. An ontology should effectively communicate the intended meaning of defined terms. Definitions should be objective and be independent of social or computational requirements.
2. Coherence. An ontology should be coherent: that is, it should sanction inferences that are consistent with definitions.
3. Extendibility: An ontology should be designed to anticipate the uses of the shared vocabulary. In other words, one should be able to define new terms for special uses based on the existing vocabulary, in a way that does not require the revision of the existing definitions.
4. Minimal encoding bias: The conceptualization should be specified at the knowledge level without depending on a particular symbol-level encoding.
5. Minimal ontological commitment: An ontology should require the minimal ontological commitment sufficient to support the intended knowledge sharing activities. That is, an ontology should make as few claims as possible about the world being modeled.

SOURCE: Adapted from Gruber (1995, p. 909).

Such metrics and guides are important detailed resources for ontology developers. The committee did not assess the many available guides, but it did identify three broad criteria for the development of an ontology—logic, validity, and usefulness—that mirror criteria used in many scientific contexts.

1. Logically sound: the ontology contains no contradictions, is technically correct, and is concisely expressed in formal terms. Historically, the verification of the consistency and correctness of an ontology has been based on metrics provided by human raters, but automated tools have recently been developed that can supplement human efforts by automatically identifying errors in the semantics and logical structure of an ontology.
2. Valid: The definitions asserted in the ontology accurately reflect what the ontology is representing and cover that domain as completely as possible. This function is dependent on human judgment, but algorithmic approaches for evaluating the accuracy and completeness of an ontology have provided new ways of assessing the validity of an ontology.
3. Useful: The ontology is usable by a diverse range of stakeholders, including social or behavioral scientists, health practitioners, and ontology developers, such as computer scientists. Assessing the usability of ontological systems is essential for developing ontologies that are easily deployed and adaptable across different contexts, and enable users to work efficiently and accurately.

THE ONTOLOGY ENGINEERING PROCESS: COMPUTATIONAL TOOLS

Since ontologies existed long before there were computers it is important to acknowledge that computational tools are not strictly necessary for ontology engineering. However, the efficiencies they provide, not to mention the capacities they afford for working with large bodies of data, have made them essential in much of behavioral science, and likely for the development and use of behavioral ontologies. Modern scientific ontologies may contain many thousands or even many millions of terms and are correspondingly complex, so technology has become essential for managing them.

Computational tools can never stand in for the human understanding, ingenuity, and social perceptions that go into the development and use of ontologies. They do not offer ready means of helping scientific communities determine what they need or of engaging colleagues in the socio-cognitive tasks detailed above. But technological tools do play an important supportive role in facilitating ontology design and use. Computational tools allow for automation of many of the operations important to ontologies, which brings valuable efficiency. Operations that can be automated include creating a subset of an ontology, importing terms from other ontologies, or verifying that all definitions in the ontology meet certain design criteria.[6] It has been proposed that artificial intelligence (AI), specifically, machine learning, could be used to support ontology development, but there is little evidence so far about its broad utility for this purpose.

A comprehensive review of available computational tools is beyond the scope of this report, but three key elements of the life-cycle of an ontology illustrate the contributions of computer technology (Noy et al., 2010):

- creating and editing the ontology;
- disseminating it so that researchers have awareness of and ready access to the ontology; and
- evaluating and debugging the ontology, in the sense of testing the logical implications of the ontologies' statements and folding findings back into the ontological structure.

Creation and Editing

Technological supports for human ideation and consensus-building are one type of computational tool that can be useful for ontology creation. Perhaps most widely used in the very early stages of ontology development is collaboration software that supports complex graphics, such as Microsoft Whiteboard. People use such tools to brainstorm ideas for what terms should be included in an ontology by suggesting competency questions, that is, questions about distinctions in the world that the ontology ought to be able to resolve (these are analogous to *requirements* in conventional software engineering). These questions help developers to flesh out the things that the ontology should encompass and stimulate developers to create an initial set of entities and relationships. Developers may also use mind mapping tools (software that supports visual structuring and organizing of complex ideas) or even simple spreadsheets to flesh out nascent ontologies. Ontology visualizations might show the meta-graph of major entity types and their linkage types to guide the selection and incorporation of existing ontologies: see Box 5-3.

Tools that make it easier to view a hierarchy of concepts, add to it, or add properties of those concepts are extremely useful in creating new ontologies and reviewing and editing existing ones. However, the possibilities for visualization on digital screens generally remain limited to tree structures,

---

[6] A good example of this capability is a collection of utilities developed by the open biological and biomedical ontology community for work in bioinformatics (Overton et al., 2015).

such as file directories. The most widely used of the tools developed for ontology editing is Protégé, an open-source system that was originally developed at Stanford University for the modeling of biomedical ontologies, and is now used in many different disciplines (Musen and Protégé Team, 2015).[7] Other tools are available: see Box 5-3. And there are commercial systems, such as TopQuadrant's TopBraid Composer[8] and OWLGrEd.[9]

These are not particularly complex technologies—they support ontology development in approximately the same way that word processing software supports the writing of a novel. A word processing program can make the writing process far more convenient and efficient than it would otherwise be, but it is of no help with the development of character and plot. Similarly, these ontology editing systems do not help elucidate the way people perceive the world.

BOX 5-3
Emerging Possibilities for Ontology Visualization

Visualization technology, first developed in the 1980s, is one of the popular techniques that focus on how to use technology to enable human understanding of ontologies and ontology-based knowledge graphs (e.g., Fairchild et al., 1988). Novel ontology visualizations make it possible to explore millions of entities and relationships, such as those in the Scalable Precision Medicine Oriented Knowledge Engine (SPOKE) graph that federates a number of open datasets into a public-data commons of health-relevant knowledge (Nelson et al., 2019; Baranzini et al., 2022).[10] SPOKE visualizations let users explore interlinked ontologies and run queries for meaningful subsets, and supports the interactive exploration of data landscapes that reveal how entities of different types are interlinked globally (providing an overview and context) and locally (via zoom-in and query).

Other emerging visualization platforms and tools include the integrated Dietary Supplements Knowledge Base (iDISK) (Rizvi et al., 2020) and the ALOHA platform designed to provide interactive visualizations of iDISK to facilitate end users' exploration and comprehension of the information in iDISK (He et al., 2019). These ontology visualization tools and methods have been shown to be somewhat helpful with exploring, navigating, and understanding the complex ontological structures for downstream use cases, such as in UFO[11] (Nguyen and Le, 2021) and ClueGo (Mlecnik et al., 2019). Nevertheless, empirical evaluation of real-world adoption of these tools with more complete analyses of their utility is needed.

---

[7] See https://protege.stanford.edu/about.php
[8] See https://www.topquadrant.com/products/topbraid-composer/
[9] See http://owlgred.lumii.lv/
[10] See https://cns-iu.github.io/spoke-vis/home and https://spoke.ucsf.edu
[11] UFO is an app that unifies most of the semantic similarity measures for between-term and between-entity similarity calculation for all types of biomedical ontologies in OBO format.

Advances in computing and algorithmic innovations can also allow for the processing of far more data than was previously possible and for increasingly sophisticated ways to identify classifications as alternative starting points for ontology creation. Statistical modeling algorithms can be used to automatically identify classes and nonlinear relationships among them, and to automatically organize very large datasets. One type of computational tool involves so-called clustering and dimensionality reduction methods (James et al., 2013; Becht et al., 2019). In different ways, these methods identify potential "groups" (perhaps based on unobserved factors) in the data. Human researchers can then assign labels or terms to the different clusters or factors (as is done for HiTOP; see Chapter 3), thereby yielding a potential set of entities for an ontology.

A concrete example of this approach, developed for characterizing psychological problems across the human life span, starts with behavioral genetic studies and infers a hierarchy of factors or dimensions that can explain psychopathology across people's lives (Lahey et al., 2017; Kotov et al., 2021).[12] The resulting entities provided a taxonomy of psychopathology and so enabled the researchers to move from a subjective categorization of psychopathology to using data for the identification of dimensions that have a causal influence on psychopathology (elements of an ontology). Historically, clustering and dimensionality reduction methods have provided either a comprehensive set of entities or information about their relationships, but not both. Statistical modeling algorithms have the potential to provide both of those parts of an ontology. In behavioral neuroscience, for instance, AI has, in recent years, largely automated the manual annotation of animals' behaviors using of video recordings. In this way, AI is used to help identify an entity for formal specification in an ontology (Mathis et al., 2018; Graving et al., 2019; Pereira et al., 2020).

The second automated approach that can aid ontology creation is to use NLP to analyze large amounts of text or documents. NLP methods can organize a body of text-based documents into topics that can be treated as a representation of the body of knowledge associated with those documents. The researchers who developed the National Cancer Institute (NCI) Thesaurus have used NLP technology developed by the National Library of Medicine (NLM), specifically the MetaMap algorithm to index text documents (Aronson, 2001; Sioutos et al., 2007; Cui et al., 2020).[13] NLM developed MetaMap with the goal of discovering meta-thesaurus concepts referred to in text. MetaMap relies heavily on NLP and other suites of

---

[12] Presentation by Benjamin Lahey to the committee during the spring 2021 workshop; see https://www.nationalacademies.org/event/05-24-2021/what-are-ontologies-and-how-are-they-used-in-science-workshop-1

[13] Presentation to the committee by Lyubov Remennik and Richard Moser during the spring 2021 workshop; see https://www.nationalacademies.org/event/06-29-2021/understanding-ontologies-in-context-workshop-2

algorithms for the statistical analysis of text data. An alternate approach, topic modeling, arguably the best known and popular form of NLP, tackles the problem of organizing text documents into topics or categories (Blei, 2012). The results can again provide an initial basis for the entities of an ontology, though human evaluation is invariably required. Ongoing research is examining how to incorporate relationships between topics into statistical models and into deep neural networks for processing text data (Gan et al., 2015).

As noted above, the people working on ontology engineering hope that formal development methods or the use of design patterns—as in conventional software engineering—will greatly facilitate the early stages of ontology development (Corcho et al., 2006). For this hope to be realized, many of these methods need to be empirically evaluated in the behavioral sciences and also built into general-purpose ontology development tools. This type of development can be guided by existing tools (e.g., ROBOT[14]) that recommend ontology design patterns or that detect the use of ontology design patterns in evolving ontologies. Further progress in the development of automated methods based on AI and machine learning that can fuse sensor and text data at scale and enable the identification of relationship between categories identified on the basis of sensor data could provide further support for ontology development. Such advances could also support the process of evaluating and reconciling different possible ontologies that can emerge from this kind of fusion.

Dissemination

Chapters 2 and 4 highlight the critical importance of making ontologies widely available and accessible, and computational tools are particularly valuable for these purposes. Available tools facilitate such tasks as searching for ontologies that contain specific terms and visualizing them. Especially important are application programming interfaces (APIs), which allow programs to access and use information from others; they depend on shared terminology. Using an API, a third-party computer program can locate terms that may be relevant for describing a scientific problem, a dataset, or some other component of interest.

For example, BioPortal, a repository of biomedical ontologies developed at Stanford University, is an open, searchable portal to which anyone can upload an ontology for distribution (Noy et al., 2009). It can recommend ontologies based on queries, analyze text documents to identify what ontology terms might be mentioned in the text, and support mapping across ontologies

---

[14] See https://robotframework.org/ also see Jackson et al. (2019).

(Whetzel and NCBO Team, 2018; Ghaazvinian, 2009).[15] BioPortal archives several hundred ontologies that are available to any user. Users who need to identify relevant ontologies among this large collection of entries for a particular purpose can use the BioPortal ontology recommender service to obtain suggestions for ontologies that may be especially appropriate for their needs (Martinez-Romero et al., 2017). Repositories for ontologies in scientific disciplines outside of biomedicine have been created using the underlying BioPortal software, which is completely domain independent. These BioPortal clones exist in various scientific domains, including materials science, ecology, and agronomy. The investigators responsible for these various discipline-specific ontology repositories have come together to form the OntoPortal Alliance.[16] Members of the Alliance develop and share software extensions to the underlying repository, and they are in discussion regarding the engineering of visualization and query components that could transcend the individual ontology repositories maintained by the group's members.

The Ontology Lookup Service (OLS) is another repository for biomedical ontologies, developed by the European Bioinformatics Institute.[17] This repository is closed, in that only ontologies approved by a team of curators are available through the site, an approach that provides greater assurance of ontology quality at the expense of benefiting from general contributions from the research community.

Evaluation and Debugging

As we note above, tools and technologies have been developed to automate and facilitate evaluation. For example, the widely used ontology software library ROBOT offers a "report" function that runs a series of quality control tests over an input ontology and generates a report file based on the results, suitable for use in an automated workflow (Jackson et al., 2019). Another emerging trend related to ontology evaluation is the increasing use of NLP to generate semantic definitions through a natural language generation task, which can parse the ontologies and generate natural language text so that humans can assess its quality.

No ontology could predict or specify every possible inference that may turn out to be wrong, but debugging an ontology—fine tuning it to eliminate errors—is challenging. In the context of ontology engineering, "debugging" is usually a matter of running a reasoner—software that can make logical inferences from information or axioms—and seeing where the reasoner makes assertions that the developer deems to be wrong and then

---

[15] See https://bioportal.bioontology.org/
[16] See https://ontoportal.org/
[17] See https://www.ebi.ac.uk/ols/index

tracking down the axioms in the ontology that led to the spurious inferences (Vrandečić, 2009; Parsia et al., 2017).

People developing ontologies in OWL, the most commonly used ontology language (see Chapter 3) take advantage of reasoners to see the logical implications of specific statements in their ontologies. Reasoners are especially useful with very large ontologies, such as the NCI Thesaurus or SNOMED,[18] to test the classifications, to make sure they are predictable, and to flag errors. Reasoners are also useful when there is uncertainty about whether the statements made by the ontology result in implications that are logically correct.

Potential Directions for the Future

The committee focused on the functions that computational tools currently provide, but there is considerable potential for future systems to provide additional kinds of support for ontology development and use. Ontology development can be quite expensive, since it requires significant people power for the intellectual work. Might technology be of use in engaging a research community in developing and evaluating ontologies collaboratively in ways that are not possible at present? Since human development and evaluation of ontologies are labor intensive, might technology be leveraged to further facilitate ontology development and evaluation, perhaps through visualization and natural language generation?

Research on ideas such as these could bring valuable developments in the long term. For example:

- One topic is improved understanding of the differences between machine and human interpretations of particular terms and between automated evaluations of ontology validity and manual reviews by human experts, as well as of hybrid systems in which humans and machines work together on ontology development, so that computational tools can be appropriately designed for human needs.
- Work could be done on ways to improve online tools to support the iterative life-cycle of ontology development and evaluation, such as ontology creation, refinement, visualization, and evaluation; more tools would be useful for automating ontology development tasks.
- Also valuable would be work on ways to leverage AI, especially machine learning, in the development and evaluation of ontologies, including application-specific efforts that reflect variability among domains.
- Another possibility is development of frameworks and scaffolding for ontology choice, not only display of ontology options as found, for example, in, the BioPortal ontology recommender.

---

[18] For more information see https://www.snomed.org/

- Another topic of interest is enhancement of ontology metadata to encode goals, past uses, organizational endorsement, and other information in a more comprehensive manner.
- It would also be valuable to have innovations that can combine AI synergistically with human intelligence to improve the development and evaluation of ontologies.

With regard to AI, current ontologies mostly capture human knowledge, but, in principle, AI-based tools could extract knowledge in an automated fashion from large datasets, such as by incorporating results from prediction models based on machine learning. For example, with data from electronic health records, one can use AI/machine learning to learn about associations between risk factors and outcomes. The finding of an association between depression and the development of dementia, for instance, could be used to populate an initial relationship in an ontology between depression and dementia. Then, AI could be used to discover and represent causal structures, evaluating an ontology from two perspectives, to determine whether the casual structures found in the data exist in the ontology, or to determine whether the asserted knowledge in the ontology agrees with an expert's knowledge.

Research on AI systems to generate both ontologies and knowledge bases, including novel hypotheses, could address challenges in efficiently creating high-quality, validated ontologies. In the medical field, for instance, physicians' reports routinely accompany the results of medical tests and images collected from patients. Taken individually, these different data modalities would result in different ontological descriptions (e.g., through knowledge embeddings) of a disease of interest. These ontological descriptions, however, ought to share some levels of similarity. This is not a trivial task. The field currently lacks a principled approach, based on AI (specifically, machine learning) for fusing knowledge embeddings and ontological descriptions obtained using different modalities. There is a need for research on multimodal data fusion and overlay with AI, and its potential use in specific contexts in the behavioral sciences.

Similarly, human-computer interaction and collaboration is currently widely studied, but rarely for the specific topic of ontologies. Research is needed on methods to translate AI-derived knowledge from large and diverse datasets into ontology elements (e.g., incorporating results from prediction models based on machine learning) and the development of novel user interfaces and data visualizations that help human users to understand and use that knowledge.

These ideas may bear fruit in the future, but we emphasize that current technology is already supporting ontology development and use and is currently more than sufficient to support progress in the behavioral sciences.

NEEDED INSTITUTIONAL AND ORGANIZATIONAL SUPPORT

Without a doubt, developing an ontology entails a lot of hard work, community engagement, and iteration. Ontology engineering is therefore a very expensive endeavor and one that requires resources as well as specific actions and processes that are sustained. It also requires continual investment because any ontology will need to evolve as the relevant science changes. Currently, there are no clear road maps for establishing and sustaining an ontology in the behavioral sciences. Many existing, well-used scientific ontologies may not be in a secure financial position, and the situation seems to be even more precarious for ontologies in the behavioral sciences.

There are a few examples of scientific ontologies that endure as robust entities. In nearly all such cases, there is a substantial commitment of government funding (or there is a government mandate to use the ontology) that ensures the durability of these resources. The NCI Thesaurus has been an intramural project at NCI for nearly three decades. The International Classification of Diseases has been managed by the World Health Organization since its inception in 1948. In contrast, financial support for efforts from university laboratories has been extremely precarious (Baker, 2012).

There is also a need for support for the tools and practices of ontology engineering. The committee believes that tools and practices developed in other contexts are likely to be valuable to behavioral scientists as they pursue ontology development, but we acknowledge that there is as yet no empirical demonstrations of how they might work in the behavioral science domain. Iterative evaluation and testing of methods applied in new contexts will need to be integrated in the broader evaluations discussed above. A wide array of changes and advancements can potentially play an important role in supporting greater reliance on ontologies in the behavioral sciences. This section outlines some key gaps and shortcomings that will need to be addressed, which fall into three categories: discovery, capacity, and practice.

Discovery

One significant need is for new information, practices, and content based on novel research and discovery. On the socio-cognitive side, additional research is needed to develop best practices for creating, disseminating, teaching, and using ontologies in the behavioral sciences. While there has been some research on best practices for ontology engineering in other domains, those techniques have not yet been widely used in the behavioral sciences. Translational research could provide important evidence about how methods in ontology engineering may need to be updated and validated for the behavioral sciences.

Similarly, both foundational and translational research is needed for the development of the next generation of computational tools that can advance the capabilities and uses of ontologies. We emphasize that the potential value of such research is not a reason to delay immediate progress in the development and use of behavioral ontologies. Nevertheless, the research directions listed above are likely to open up new possibilities.

Capacity

Shortfalls in implementation, and the capacity for implementation, of approaches whose value has already been demonstrated also need to be addressed. When what needs to be done is clear—and additional research is not needed—but the resources or capacity to do it are not currently available, progress is hampered. There is a need for additional resources to increase awareness and training regarding ontologies in the behavioral sciences. There are many individuals in library and information sciences, for example, who have experience with ontology creation and use in other domains but may not have opportunities or time to work with behavioral scientists. Other fields have developed mechanisms to train scientists in ontology-relevant approaches, such as informatics, as exemplified in the partnership of the National Institute of Dental and Craniofacial Research with NLM on continuing education training (T15) grants. At the same time, many of the relevant stakeholders in behavioral sciences may not have the computational training or the skills needed to work with ontologies and the relevant tools, and will thus need additional computational training or support. In addition, full utilization of both current and future computational tools will require significant increases in computational resources including computer time, data access, and server storage. Institutions and organizations will also likely require additional resources, particularly if they play increasingly prominent roles in the development, dissemination, and use of ontologies (as suggested by the success of the NCI Thesaurus).

Practices

A final set of needs involves practices and processes that could support wider use of ontologies in the behavioral sciences for which the capacity is already in place. As noted above, there are currently few explicit institutional incentives to use ontologies in the behavioral sciences, whether from journals, conferences, funding agencies, review committees, or other entities. Open data and code have become much more widespread as relevant institutions have required them. The movement toward open science depends on the existence of ontologies to enable comparisons between datasets, and recent trends in expectations for data sharing are changing this situation. Funders and publishers now often require data sharing, which requires the use of standardized metadata, which in turn requires the use of ontologies. But there have as yet been comparatively few community-level efforts to build consensus about the use of ontologies in the behavioral sciences: there are many ways to encourage this, as we propose in Chapter 6. There are no perfect or completed ontologies, regardless of domain; ontologies are always subject to revision as the scientific community learns and changes. Nonetheless, experiences in other domains have shown that consensus around an ontology is possible, though it requires concerted efforts by researchers and institutions.

CONCLUSIONS

CONCLUSION 5-1: Valuable ontological systems and related tools exist and are supporting research in the behavioral sciences. However, many of these efforts have been isolated, and it appears that their adoption has been constrained; that resources to support them (including training and education) have been limited; and that the developers of ontological systems are largely on their own to identify or develop the models, tools, and approaches that might best advance research and practice.

CONCLUSION 5-2: Ontology engineering rests on two foundations: socio-cognitive functions through which decisions about terms and their relationships are made and computational tools that support the overall process, providing both efficiencies and techniques for working with large bodies of data.

CONCLUSION 5-3: To provide the intended benefits an ontology should be logically sound, valid, and usable:

- logically sound—contains no contradictions and is technically correct and concisely expressed in formal terms;
- valid—the definitions it provides accurately reflect the domain it covers as completely as possible; and
- usable by a diverse range of stakeholders, depending on its purpose—including scientists, practitioners, and others.

CONCLUSION 5-4: For ontology engineering to progress in the behavioral sciences, sustained resources and specific actions and processes are needed in three areas:

- *discovery* both foundational and translational research needed to develop and improve effective practices and the next generation of computational tools for ontology engineering in the behavioral sciences.

- *capacity* to address shortfalls in implementation and to take advantage of the cases when novel research is not required—that is, when what needs to be done is clear, but there is currently no capacity to do it.
- *promotion of practices and processes* that could support wider use of ontologies in the behavioral sciences, and for which the capacity is already in place, but have not been widely deployed, such as institutional incentives, open data and code, and community-level efforts to bring consensus about ontologies in the behavioral sciences through collaboration.

REFERENCES

Amith, M., He, Z., Bian, J., Lossio-Ventura, J. A., and Tao, C. (2018). Assessing the practice of biomedical ontology evaluation: Gaps and opportunities. *Journal of Biomedical Informatics*, 80, 1–13. https://doi.org/10.1016/j.jbi.2018.02.010

Aronson, A.R. (2001). Effective mapping of biomedical text to the UMLS Metathesaurus: the MetaMap program. In *Proceedings of the AMIA Symposium*, 17. American Medical Informatics Association. https://www.ncbi.nlm.nih.gov/pmc/articles/PMC2243666/

Baker, M. (2012). Databases fight funding cuts. *Nature*, 489(7414), 19. https://doi.org/10.1038/489019a

Baranzini, S.E., Börner, K., Morris, J., Nelson, C.A., Soman, K., Schleimer, E., Keiser, M., Musen, M., Pearce, R., Reza, T., Smith, B., Herr, B., Oskotsky, B., Rizk-Jackson, A., Rankin, K.P., Sanders, S.J., Bove, R., Rose, P.W., Israni, S., and Huang, S. (2022). A biomedical open knowledge network harnesses the power of AI to understand deep human biology. *AI Magazine*, 41(1), 46–58. https://doi.org/10.1002/aaai.12037

Becht, E., McInnes, L., Healy, J., Dutertre, C.A., Kwok, I.W., Ng, L.G., Ginhoux, F, and Newell, E.W. (2019). Dimensionality reduction for visualizing single-cell data using UMAP. *Nature Biotechnology*, 37(1), 38–44. https://doi.org/10.1038/nbt.4314

Benmimoune, L., Hajjam, A., Ghodous, P., Andres, E., Talha, S., and Hajjam, M. (2015). Ontology-based medical decision support system to enhance chronic patients' lifestyle within E-care telemonitoring platform. *Studies in Health Technology and Informatics*, 213, 279–282

Bickmore, T.W., Schulman, D., and Sidner, C.L. (2011). A reusable framework for health counseling dialogue systems based on a behavioral medicine ontology. *Journal of Biomedical Informatics*, 44(2), 183–197. https://doi.org/10.1016/j.jbi.2010.12.006

Blanch, A., García, R., Planes, J., Gil, R., Balada, F., Blanco, E., and Aluja, A. (2017). Ontologies about human behavior: A review of knowledge modeling systems. *European Psychologist*, 22(3), 180–197. https://doi.org/10.1027/1016-9040/a000295

Blaum, W.E., Jarczweski, A., Balzer, F., Stötzner, P., and Ahlers, O. (2013). Towards Web 3.0: Taxonomies and ontologies for medical education—a systematic review. *GMS Zeitschrift fur Medizinische Ausbildung*, 30(1), Doc13. https://doi.org/10.3205/zma000856

Blei, D. M. (2012). Probabilistic topic models. *Communications of the ACM*, 55(4), 77–84. https://doi.org/10.1145/2133806.2133826

Blomqvist, E., and Sandkuhl, K. (2005). Patterns in ontology engineering: Classification of ontology patterns. In C.-S. Chen, J. Filipe, I. Seruca, and J. Cordeiro (Eds.), *ICEIS 2005: Proceedings of the seventh International Conference on Enterprise Information Systems*, May 25–28, 2005, 413–416. https://www.scitepress.org/PublicationsDetail.aspx?ID=D81zWiWWmYE=&t=1

Brenas, J.H., Shin, E. K., and Shaban-Nejad, A. (2019). Adverse Childhood Experiences Ontology for mental health surveillance, research, and evaluation: Advanced knowledge representation and Semantic Web techniques. *JMIR Mental Health,* 6(5), e13498. https://doi.org/10.2196/13498

Brochhausen, M., Spear, A.D., Cocos, C., Weiler, G., Martín, L., Anguita, A., Stenzhorn, H., Daskalaki, E., Schera, F., Schwarz, U., Sfakianakis, S., Kiefer, S., Dörr, M., Graf, N., and Tsiknakis, M. (2011). The ACGT Master Ontology and its applications—Towards an ontology-driven cancer research and management system. *Journal of Biomedical Informatics,* 44(1), 8–25. https://doi.org/10.1016/j.jbi.2010.04.008

Corcho, O., Fernández-López, M., and Gómez-Pérez, A. (2006). Ontological engineering: Principles, methods, tools and languages. In C. Calero, F. Ruiz, and M. Piattini (Eds.), *Ontologies for Software Engineering and Software Technology,* 1–48. Berlin: Springer Berlin Heidelberg. https://doi.org/10.1007/3-540-34518-3_1

Crandall, B., Klein, G.A., and Hoffman, R.R. (2006). *Working Minds: A Practitioner's Guide to Cognitive Task Analysis.* Cambridge, MA: MIT Press.

Cui, L., Abeysinghe, R., Zheng, F., Tao, S., Zeng, N., Hands, I., Durbin, E.B., Whiteman, L., Remennik, L., Sioutos, N., and Zhang, G.Q. (2020). Enhancing the quality of hierarchic relations in the National Cancer Institute Thesaurus to enable faceted query of cancer registry data. *Journal of Clinical Ontology Clinical Cancer Informatics,* 4, 392–398. https://doi.org/10.1200/CCI.19.00124

Eisenberg, I.W., Bissett, P.G., Canning, J.R., Dallery, J., Enkavi, A.Z., Whitfield-Gabrieli, S., Gonzalez, O., Green, A.I., Greene, M.A., Kiernan, M., Kim, S.J., Li, J., Lowe, M.R., Mazza, G.L., Metcalf, S.A., Onken, L., Parikh, S.S., Peters, E., Prochaska, J.J., Scherer, E.A., Stoeckel, L.E., Valente, M.J., Wu, J., Xie, H., MacKinnon, D.P., Marsch, L.A., and Poldrack, R.A. (2018). Applying novel technologies and methods to inform the ontology of self-regulation. *Behaviour Research and Therapy,* 101, 46–57. https://doi.org/10.1016/j.brat.2017.09.014

Fairchild, K.M., Poltrock, S.E., and Furnas, G.W. (1988). SemNet: Three-dimensional graphic representation of large knowledge bases. In Guidon, R. (Ed.), *Cognitive Science and its Applications for Human-Computer Interaction,* 201–234. Hillsdale, NJ: Lawrence Erlbaum Associates, Hillsdale, N.J.

Falzon, L. (2021). *Scoping Review of Ontologies in the Behavioral Sciences.* Paper prepared for the Committee on Accelerating Behavioral Science Through Ontology Development and Use, National Academies of Sciences, Engineering, and Medicine. https://nap.nationalacademies.org/resource/26464/Falzon-comissioned-paper.pdf

Franco, M., Vivo, J.M., Quesada-Martínez, M., Duque-Ramos, A., and Fernández-Breis, J.T. (2020). Evaluation of ontology structural metrics based on public repository data. *Briefings in Bioinformatics,* 21(2), 473–485. https://doi.org/10.1093/bib/bbz00

Gan, Z., Chen, C., Henao, R., Carlson, D., and Carin, L. (2015). Scalable deep Poisson factor analysis for topic modeling. In *International Conference on Machine Learning,* 1823–1832. Proceedings of Machine Learning Research.

Ghaazvinian, A., Noy, N.F., and Musen, M.A. (2009). Creating mappings for ontologies in biomedicine: Simple methods work. *AMIA Annual Symposium Proceedings, 2009,* 198–202. https://pubmed.ncbi.nlm.nih.gov/20351849/

Gkoutos, G.V., Hoehndorf, R., Tsaprouni, L., and Schofield, P.N. (2015). Best behaviour? Ontologies and the formal description of animal behaviour. *Mammalian Genome,* 26(9-10), 540–547.

Gkoutos, G.V., Schofield, P.N., and Hoehndorf, R. (2012). The neurobehavior ontology: An ontology for annotation and integration of behavior and behavioral phenotypes. *International Review of Neurobiology,* 103, 69–87. https://doi.org/10.1016/B978-0-12-388408-4.00004-6

Graving, J.M., Chae, D., Naik, H., Li, L., Koger, B., Costelloe, B.R., and Couzin, I.D. (2019). DeepPoseKit, a software toolkit for fast and robust animal pose estimation using deep learning. *eLife*, e47994. https://doi.org/10.7554/eLife.47994

Gruber, T.R. (1995). Toward principles for the design of ontologies used for knowledge sharing? *International Journal of Human-Computer Studies, 43*(5–6), 907–928. https://doi.org/10.1006/ijhc.1995.1081

Hastings, J., and Schultz, S. (2012). Ontologies for human behavior analysis and their application to clinical cata. In E.M. Chesler and M.A. Haendel, Eds. *Bioinformatics of Behavior: Part 1, 103*, 89–107. Amsterdam, The Netherlands: Elsevier.

He, X., Zhang, R., Rizvi, R., Vasilakes, J., Yang, X., Guo, Y., He, Z., Prosperi, M., Huo, J., Alpert, J., and Bian, J. (2019). ALOHA: Developing an interactive graph-based visualization for dietary supplement knowledge graph through user-centered design. *BMC Medical Informatics and Decision Making, 19*(Suppl 4), 150. https://doi.org/10.1186/s12911-019-0857-1

Hicks, A., Hanna, J., Welch, D., Brochhausen, M., and Hogan, W.R. (2016). The ontology of medically related social entities: Recent developments. *Journal of Biomedical Semantics, 7*, 47. https://doi.org/10.1186/s13326-016-0087-8

Hitzler, P., Gangemi, A., and Janowicz, K. (Eds.). (2016). *Ontology Engineering with Ontology Design Patterns: Foundations and applications, 25*. Amsterdam, The Netherlands: IOS Press.

Hollnagel, E. (Ed.). (2003). *Handbook of Cognitive Task Design*. Boca Raton, FL: CRC Press.

Jackson, R.C., Balhoff, J.P., Douglass, E., Harris, N.L., Mungall, C.J., and Overton, J.A. (2019). ROBOT: A tool for automating ontology workflows. *BMC Bioinformatics, 20*(1), 407. https://doi.org/10.1186/s12859-019-3002-3

Jackson, R., Matentzoglu, N., Overton, J.A., Vita, R., Balhoff, J.P., Buttigieg, P.L., Carbon, S., Courtot, M., Diehl, A.D., Dooley, D.M., Duncan, W.D., Harris, N.L., Haendel, M.A., Lewis, S.E., Natale, D.A., Osumi-Sutherland, D., Ruttenberg, A., Schriml, L.M., Smith, B., Stoeckert, C. J., Jr, Vasilevsky, N.A., Walls, R.L., Zheng, J., Mungall, C.J., and Peters, B. (2021). OBO Foundry in 2021: Operationalizing open data principles to evaluate ontologies. *Database: The Journal of Biological Databases and Curation, 2021*, baab069. https://doi.org/10.1093/database/baab069

James, G., Witten, D., Hastie, T., and Tibshirani, R. (2013). *An Introduction to Statistical Learning*. New York: Springer.

Jensen, M., Cox, A.P., Chaudhry, N., Ng, M., Sule, D., Duncan, W., Ray, P., Weinstock-Guttman, B., Smith, B., Ruttenberg, A., Szigeti, K., and Diehl, A.D. (2013). The neurological disease ontology. *Journal of Biomedical Semantics, 4*(1), 42.

Jung, H., Park, H.A., and Song, T.M. (2016). Development and evaluation of an adolescents' depression ontology for analyzing social data. *Studies in Health Technology and Informatics, 225*, 442–446.

Kanopka, B.M. (2015). Biomedical ontologies—A review. *Biocybernetics and Biomedical Engineering, 35*(2), 75–86.

Köhler, S., Doelken, S.C., Rath, A., Aymé, S., and Robinson, P.N. (2012). Ontological phenotype standards for neurogenetics. *Human Mutation, 33*(9), 1333–1339.

Kotov, R., Krueger, R.F., Watson, D., Cicero, D.C., Conway, C.C., DeYoung, C.G., Eaton, N.R., Forbes, M.K., Hallquist, M.N., Latzman, R.D., Mullins-Sweatt, S.N., Ruggero, C.J., Simms, L.J., Waldman, I.D., Waszczuk, M.A., and Wright, A. (2021). The Hierarchical Taxonomy of Psychopathology (HiTOP): A quantitative nosology based on consensus of evidence. *Annual Review of Clinical Psychology, 17*, 83–108. https://doi.org/10.1146/annurev-clinpsy-081219-093304

Lahey, B.B., Krueger, R.F., Rathouz, P.J., Waldman, I.D., and Zald, D.H. (2017). A hierarchical causal taxonomy of psychopathology across the life span. *Psychological Bulletin, 143*, (2), 142–186. https://doi.org/10.1037/bul0000069

Larsen, K.R., Michie, S., Hekler, E.B., Gibson, B., Spruijt-Metz, D., Ahern, D., Cole-Lewis, H., Ellis, R.J., Hesse, B., Moser, R.P., and Yi, J. (2017). Behavior change interventions: The potential of ontologies for advancing science and practice. *Journal of Behavioral Medicine*, 40(1), 6–22. https://doi.org/10.1007/s10865-016-9768-0

Lokker, C., McKibbon, K.A., Colquhoun, H., and Hempel, S. (2015). A scoping review of classification schemes of interventions to promote and integrate evidence into practice in healthcare. *Implementation Science*, 10, 27. https://doi.org/10.1186/s13012-015-0220-6

Martinez-Romero, M., Jonquet, C., O'Connor, M.J., Graybeal, J., Pazos, A., and Musen, M.A. (2017). NCBO Ontology Recommender 2.0: An enhanced approach for biomedical ontology recommendation. *Journal of Biomedical Semantics*, 8(1), 21. https://doi.org/10.1186/s13326-017-0128-y

Mathis, A., Mamidanna, P., Cury, K.M., Abe, T., Murthy, V.N., Mathis, M.W., and Bethge, M. (2018). DeepLabCut: Markerless pose estimation of user-defined body parts with deep learning. *Nature Neuroscience*, 21(9), 1281–1289. https://doi.org/10.1038/s41593-018-0209-y

Mlecnik, B., Galon, J., and Bindea, G. (2019). Automated exploration of gene ontology term and pathway networks with ClueGO-REST. *Bioinformatics (Oxford, England)*, 35(19), 3864–3866. https://doi.org/10.1093/bioinformatics/btz163

Musen, M., and Protégé Team. (2015). The Protégé Project: A look back and look forward. *AI Matters*, 1(4), 4–12. https://doi.org/10.1145/2757001.2757003

Nelson, C.A., Butte, A.J., and Baranzini, S.E. (2019). Integrating biomedical research and electronic health records to create knowledge-based biologically meaningful machine-readable embeddings. *Nature Communications*, 10(1), 3045. https://doi.org/10.1038/s41467-019-11069-0

Nguyen, Q.H., and Le, D.H. (2021). Similarity calculation, enrichment analysis, and ontology visualization of biomedical ontologies using UFO. *Current Protocols*, 1(4), e115. https://doi.org/10.1002/cpz1.115

Norris, E., Finnerty, A.N., Hastings, J., Stokes, G., and Michie, S. (2019). A scoping review of ontologies related to human behaviour change. *Nature Human Behaviour*, 3(2), 164–172. https://doi.org/10.1038/s41562-018-0511-4

Norris, E., Hastings, J., Marques, M.M., Mutlu, A., Zink, S., and Michie, S. (2021). Why and how to engage expert stakeholders in ontology development: Insights from social and behavioural sciences. *Journal of Biomedical Semantics*, 12(1), 4. https://doi.org/10.1186/s13326-021-00240-6

Noy, N.F., Shah, N.H., Whetzel, P.L., Dai, B., Dorf, M., Griffith, N., Jonquet, C., Rubin, D.L., Storey, M.A., Chute, C.G., and Musen, M.A. (2009). BioPortal: Ontologies and integrated data resources at the click of a mouse. *Nucleic Acids Research*, 37(Suppl-2), W170–W173. https://doi.org/10.1093/nar/gkp440

Noy, N., Tudorache, T., Nyulas, C., and Musen, M. (2010). The ontology life cycle: Integrated tools for editing, publishing, peer review, and evolution of ontologies. *AMIA Annual Symposium Proceedings*, 2010, 552–556.

Obrst, L., Ceusters, W., Mani, I., Ray, S., and Smith, B. (2007). The evaluation of ontologies: Toward improved semantic interoperability. *Semantic Web: Revolutionizing Knowledge Discovery in the Life Sciences*, 139–158. https://www.researchgate.net/publication/225855591_The_Evaluation_of_Ontologies

Overton, J.A., Dietze, H., Essaid, S., Osumi-Sutherland, D., and Mungall, C.J. (2015). ROBOT: A command-line tool for ontology development. *International Conference on Biomedical Ontologies*. http://icbo2015.fc.ul.pt/demo6.pdf

Parsia, B., Matentzoglu, N., Gonçalves, R.S., Glimm, B., and Steigmiller, A. (2017). The OWL Reasoner Evaluation (ORE) 2015 competition report. *Journal of Automated Reasoning*, 59(4), 455–482. https://doi.org/10.1007/s10817-017-9406-8

Pereira, T.D., Shaevitz, J.W., and Murthy, M. (2020). Quantifying behavior to understand the brain. *Nature Neuroscience*, 23(12), 1537–1549. https://doi.org/10.1038/s41593-020-00734-z

Poldrack, R., and Yarkoni, T. (2016). From brain maps to cognitive ontologies: Informatics and the search for mental structure. *Annual Review of Psychology*, 67, 587–612. https://doi.org/10.1146/annurev-psych-122414-033729

Rensselaer Polytechnic Institute. (2013). The general ontology evaluation framework (GOEF): A proposed infrastructure for the ontology development lifecycle. http://ontolog.cim3.net/file/work/OntologySummit2013/2013-03-14_OntologySummit2013_Ontology Evaluation-Quality-Methodology-2/OntologySummit2013_GOEF_iChoose—Joanne Luciano_20130314.pdf

Rizvi, R., Vasilakes, J., Adam, T.J., Melton, G.B., Bishop, J.R., Bian, J., Tao, C., and Zhang, R. (2020). iDISK: The Integrated Dietary Supplements Knowledge Base. *Journal of the American Medical Informatics Association*, 27(4), 539–548. https://doi.org/10.1093/jamia/ocz216

Sioutos, N., de Coronado, S., Haber, M.W., Hartel, F.W., Shaiu, W.L., and Wright, L.W. (2007). NCI Thesaurus: A semantic model integrating cancer-related clinical and molecular information. *Journal of Biomedical Informatics*, 40(1), 30–43. https://doi.org/10.1016/j.jbi.2006.02.013

Stancin, K., Poscic, P., and Jaksic, D. (2020). Ontologies in education—state of the art. *Education and Information Technologies*, 25(6), 5301–5320.

Vrandečić, D. (2009). Ontology evaluation. In S. Staab and R. Studer (Eds.), *Handbook on Ontologies*. Springer. https://doi.org/10.1007/978-3-540-92673-3_13

Whetzel, P., and NCBO Team. (2013). NCBO technology: Powering semantically aware applications. *Journal of Biomedical Semantics*, 4(Suppl 1), S8. https://doi.org/10.1186/2041-1480-4-S1-S8

Win, K.T., Ramaprasad, A., and Syn, T. (2019). Ontological Review of Persuasion Support Systems (PSS) for Health Behavior Change through Physical Activity. *Journal of Medical Systems*, 43(3), 49. https://doi.org/10.1007/s10916-019-1159-y

Woznowski, P.R., Tonkin, E.L., and Flach, P.A. (2018). Activities of Daily Living Ontology for Ubiquitous Systems: Development and Evaluation. *Sensors*, 18(7):20.

Wu, H., and Yamaguchi, A. (2014). Semantic Web technologies for the big data in life sciences. *Bioscience Trends*, 8(4), 192–201. https://doi.org/10.5582/bst.2014.01048

Yao, L., Divoli, A., Mayzus, I., Evans, J.A., and Rzhetsky, A. (2011). Benchmarking ontologies: Bigger or better? *PLoS Computational Biology*, 7(1), e1001055.

Yu, C., and Shen, B. (2016). XML, ontologies, and their clinical applications. *Advances in Experimental Medicine and Biology*, 939, 259–287. https://doi.org/10.1007/978-981-10-1503-8_11

Zhu, Q., Kong, X., Hong, S., Li, J., and He, Z. (2015). Global ontology research progress: A bibliometric analysis. *Aslib Journal of Information Management*, 67(1), 27–54.

6

Conclusions and Recommendations

The committee considered ontologies from multiple perspectives. To address our charge, we explored individual ontologies, reviewed longstanding philosophical issues, and reviewed literature on behavioral ontologies and on computer technology that can support their development and use. We sought to answer four basic questions:

- What problems in behavioral science might be remedied or mitigated by ontologies?
- What, precisely, are ontologies and how do they differ from other knowledge structures?
- Why are ontologies so important to advancement in the behavioral sciences?
- How can the engineering of ontologies in the behavioral sciences be strengthened?

Based on our analysis of those four questions, we offer nine conclusions about how ontologies could accelerate progress in the behavioral sciences and how to engineer them. And, based on those conclusions, we offer six recommendations to those who fund, influence, and carry out research about how to stimulate and provide support for ontology development.

THE NEED FOR ONTOLOGIES IN THE BEHAVIORAL SCIENCES

Ontologies provide a structure for the entities in a domain: they articulate conceptualizations, or descriptions of the nature of the ideas under study, and connections among those concepts, such as a set of relationships. They are a means of reliably specifying and classifying behavioral phenomena; providing a controlled vocabulary for discussion of research; and identifying the inconsistent use of definitions, labels, relations among entities, and measures. Thus, they provide the basis for sharing knowledge about the entities in a domain across diverse approaches and methodologies. In addition, ontologies facilitate the generation, curation, dissemination, and retrieval of knowledge by supporting the codification of research findings in computer-readable formats (Larsen et al., 2017). Thus, ontologies can address problems with research itself and with its application to real-world problems.

A wide variety of stakeholders rely on the knowledge created by the behavioral sciences, including, just in the domain of mental health, scientists who study behavior, social science, psychology, development, and cognition; and clinicians who provide educational, behavioral, social, and psychological interventions; as well as educators, health care practitioners, policy makers, and patients. One in five adults experiences a mental condition in a given year, and the quality of their care depends on both the availability of research on mental disorders and the capacity of clinicians to distill relevant information from the massive volume of research published every year. For new knowledge to benefit patients, clinicians, and communities, it must be tested and reproduced, and the findings must be integrated with other knowledge, synthesized, generalized, disseminated, and applied. The overwhelming cascade of new research makes it difficult to synthesize results, and ontologies offer an infrastructure for systematically organizing and sorting research findings in particular domains so that key developments can easily be discerned by those who rely on them.

The absence of ontologies also undermines research itself; a lack of ontological clarity is at the root of many significant challenges faced by behavioral scientists. Scientists' work is shaped by their understanding of the concepts and entities they are studying and how they are categorized, decisions about ways to accurately measure the phenomena of interest, and decisions about what is and is not germane to their research investigations. Today, the mapping or documentation of relationships among measures, terms, and entities remains fragmented and scattered across many fields within the behavioral, social, and cognitive sciences. These problems are manifested in poor generalizability of many research findings, which results in behavioral science research findings that do not build cumulatively to the degree that they could. Ontological specifications that are interoperable—useful across applications because they provide formal consistent, computable, and readily re-purposed specifications—can yield cost savings, efficiencies, and opportunities across research needs and applications.

We could not find clear empirical evidence that the absence of publicly available, agreed-upon ontologies has limited progress in the behavioral sciences or that deficiencies in ontologies and common vocabularies by themselves have limited cumulative progress in these fields. It is nonetheless clear from our review that the behavioral sciences are not characterized by robust ontologies, and that the lack of ontologies can hinder scientific progress. To remind the reader of just one example (from Chapter 3), the Behaviour Change Intervention Ontology (BCIO) was designed to address the problem posed by theories that were overlapping and underspecified, often sharing constructs with other theories, using different names for the same constructs, measuring the same constructs using differing items, and inadequately defining constructs and relationships.

We reviewed a number of existing ontological systems in the behavioral sciences, including ones that might fall at various points along a continuum of semantic formality (discussed in Chapter 3) and some that we were not able to clearly characterize in those terms. It may be that some domains of the behavioral sciences have more to gain from a focus on ontology development than others. Nevertheless, while existing ontological systems have served valuable purposes, taken together they have not exploited the large potential for ontologies to accelerate advancement and application of behavioral research. Our scoping review and examination of example ontological systems indicated that there are comparatively few semantically formal behavioral science ontologies. Many of the systems that have been developed to support research are not likely to bring the full benefits that a clear ontology can offer, and the systems that appear to have been most explicitly designed with ontological goals in mind (e.g., BCIO, Cognitive Atlas) are not widely used. A systematic exploration of why this is so was beyond our reach: the available literature provides few generalizable insights, and our investigation of the examples we did look at suggested that the reasons are complex.

> **CONCLUSION 3-1:** Classification systems in the behavioral sciences lie on a continuum of semantic specification. Systems that fall along this continuum serve ontological purposes that are scientifically valuable.

> **CONCLUSION 3-2:** The classification systems that currently are widely used in the behavioral sciences do not have formal semantics, and therefore they do not readily provide opportunities to support automated reasoning and other artificial intelligence applications.

> **CONCLUSION 3-3:** While ontological systems with the most formal semantic specification offer the greatest opportunities for accelerating the behavioral sciences through the use of artificial intelligence, it is not the case that the continuum represents a hierarchy of quality. The most important characteristic of an ontological system is that its level of formal specificity fits its intended purpose.

CONCLUSION 4-1: By establishing a controlled vocabulary of shared terms for the concepts and phenomena of interest in a particular domain and a classification of those entities, ontological systems have three primary benefits:

- They open up opportunities to improve care and services, based on the work of investigators studying disorders who use a common language, shared measures, and the same logical structure for designing their specific studies.
- They provide an infrastructure to support the mechanics and application of contemporary scientific research, helping to ensure that conclusions drawn from the data are justified, the procedures used to create the data are replicable, and new discoveries buried in the data do not go undiscovered; framing communication between people and machines; easing the interpretation of complex datasets; and making scientific data an enduring and available resource for all.
- They create enhanced capacity to expand scientific knowledge, providing a foundation for thought, hypotheses, and understanding of new discoveries.

STRENGTHENING ONTOLOGY USE IN THE BEHAVIORAL SCIENCES

What would it take to achieve the potential benefits we have described? We believe that behavioral science can learn from other fields, such as cancer research and anatomy, where formal ontologies have been developed and currently serve the function of standardizing information and organizing knowledge. The U.S. research community can also learn from the ways ontology development and use are funded and supported in other countries; though reviewing international approaches was beyond our scope, we are aware that researchers outside the United States have been leaders in ontology development.

In attempting to understand what would be needed to engineer ontologies that could better support behavioral science, we examined socio-cognitive practices or functions through which decisions about the terms and relationships the ontology covers are made and the computational tools that can facilitate the intellectual work.

The socio-cognitive practices involved in creating and editing an ontology and adapting it over time require intensive human community engagement, and iteration. Computer tools—including software that supports collaboration and brainstorming, makes it easier to visualize complex relationships, and facilitates sharing and disseminating ontologies—can bring extremely valuable efficiency to the development, maintenance, and editing of ontologies. Statistical methods that identify common factors and hierarchical organizations among correlated behavioral measures can also support ontology development. But these tools can never stand in for the human understanding, ingenuity, establishment of consensus, and leadership that go into the development and use of ontologies. Because of the basic need for human work, ontology development is quite expensive. There is no substitute for the raw people power that is essential for the intellectual work of designing the ontology.

CONCLUSION 5-1: Valuable ontological systems and related tools exist and are supporting research in the behavioral sciences. However, many of these efforts have been isolated, and it appears that their adoption has been constrained; that resources to support them (including training and education) have been limited; and that the developers of ontological systems are largely on their own to identify or develop the models, tools, and approaches that might best advance research and practice.

CONCLUSION 5-2: Ontology engineering rests on two foundations: socio-cognitive functions through which decisions about terms and their relationships are made and computational tools that support the overall process, providing both efficiencies and techniques for working with large bodies of data.

CONCLUSION 5-3: To provide the intended benefits, an ontology should be logically sound, valid, and usable:

- logically sound—contains no contradictions and is technically correct and concisely expressed in formal terms;
- valid—the definitions it provides accurately reflect the domain it covers as completely as possible; and
- usable by a diverse range of stakeholders, depending on its purpose, including scientists, practitioners, and others.

CONCLUSION 5-4: For ontology engineering to progress in the behavioral sciences, sustained resources and specific actions and processes are needed in three areas:

- *discovery* both foundational and translational research needed to develop and improve effective practices and the next generation of computational tools for ontology engineering in the behavioral sciences.

- *capacity* to address shortfalls in implementation and to take advantage of the cases when novel research is not required—that is, when what needs to be done is clear, but there is currently no capacity to do it.
- *promotion of practices and processes* that could support wider use of ontologies in the behavioral sciences, and for which the capacity is already in place, but have not been widely deployed, such as institutional incentives, open data and code, and community-level efforts to bring consensus about ontologies in the behavioral sciences through collaboration.

SUPPORTING AND SUSTAINING BEHAVIORAL ONTOLOGIES

The committee recognizes that some behavioral scientists remain skeptical of the usefulness of ontologies despite their potential benefits. Skeptics argue that ontologies may have the unintended consequence of stifling research creativity or that the imposition of a common ontology could make it more difficult for new conceptualizations to gain a foothold. The committee acknowledges that there may be complicated tradeoffs and that too much emphasis on a common ontological system could hinder originality and punish some of the unorthodox thinking that has led to major scientific advances. In assessing this concern, however, the committee notes that many scientific disciplines rely on ontologies to a far greater extent than do the behavioral sciences, and it would be hard to argue that research in those sciences is less creative than that in the behavioral sciences. What we are proposing is fundamentally consistent with long-standing reliance on constructs, construct validity, and other means of clearly articulating ideas and hypotheses for rigorous study. A greater reliance on ontologies is a way of making those efforts even more rigorous.

Moreover, the committee expects that increased use of ontologies in the behavioral sciences would involve different and sometimes parallel ontologies. The methods for developing ontologies vary, and the creation of categories depends on human judgment. Differences of opinion should be expected. Especially in the near term, "ontologic pluralism"—in which competing or overlapping ontologies exist and are connected to one another through formal mappings—is both inevitable and desirable. Without a doubt, however, developing workable ontologies is difficult, though it is necessary in any scientific domain.

CONCLUSION 6-1: Ontology development and use has the potential to move behavioral science forward from a domain in which research is generally siloed and the data and results are often incompatible to one in which the evidence is searchable and more easily integrated and in which computer technology is leveraged in the discovery of new relationships, the development of novel hypotheses, and the identification of knowledge gaps.

Taking advantage of these opportunities to accelerate the behavioral sciences with the aid of more semantically formal ontologies will require attention to the practical challenges of supporting the needed work. There are only a few examples of behavioral science ontologies that have endured. A primary—perhaps the most important—reason for this situation is that the development and maintenance of ontologies is expensive. Despite the many efficiencies afforded by computer technology, developing an ontology is a painstaking effort. Particularly within the behavioral sciences there has been a lack of sustainable resources: ontology development does not usually lead to a commercial product.

As a result, some ontological systems have been supported by national or international agencies. For example, the International Classification of Diseases has been supported by the World Health Organization because it is essential for public health surveillance. The Diagnostic and Statistical Manual of Mental Disorders has been supported by the American Psychiatric Association because it is the basis for billing for psychiatric and psychological services. The National Institutes of Health (NIH) has devoted intramural funds for ontologies and related resources, including the National Cancer Institute (NCI) Thesaurus, the Medical Subject Headings of the National Library of Medicine (NLM), and the structure that underlies ClinicalTrials.gov.

However, continuing support for nongovernmental efforts has been limited. The most widely used open-source ontology development system, Protégé, has pieced together funding from NLM, NCI, the National Institute of General Medical Sciences, the National Science Foundation, the Defense Advanced Research Projects Agency, and other organizations through limited research grants and contracts. While the project currently has short-term support from its various public and private sponsors, it is not on a sure financial footing for the future. Strategies to supplement long-term agency investments in infrastructure for research exist: see Box 6-1. Such examples are suggestive, but fee-generating structures will not be appropriate for all areas of research, and it is clear that without sustained resources for ontologies, the behavioral sciences are not likely to take advantage of what they can offer.

CONCLUSION 6-2: Although ontologies are central to the advancement of science, there are no existing funding mechanisms for the development and maintenance of such systems and for the tools that support them. Sustained public and private support for the long-term development, dissemination, and maintenance of ontologies in the behavioral sciences and related tools is needed.

For the behavioral sciences to benefit from the potential advantages of well-designed ontologies, an infrastructure is also needed. In developing

> **BOX 6-1**
> **Example of Agency Investment**
>
> The NIH Common Fund supported PROMIS®, an effort to develop common measures of patient reported outcomes for use in medical research and practice. NIH supported the effort from 2004 to 2014 as part of an effort to establish tools that would be freely available for research investigators and others, with funding sources. NIH provided a 4-year award to Northwestern University to build an infrastructure for open access to the PROMIS® item banks, but fee-generating structures were also developed that provided enough support to sustain ongoing PROMIS® activities. These included licensing of item response theory-based scoring methods that were available for a distribution fee and paying memberships in an organization that offers workshops and other benefits related to the use of PROMIS®.
>
> SOURCE: Based on information in Cella and Hays (2021).

its recommendations about this need, the committee weighed competing perspectives about what would be most helpful. It might be reasonable to suppose that an infrastructure that could, in effect, govern the development and use of ontologies in the behavioral sciences to ensure that the effort to substantially expand their use would provide the requisite consistency and support. In that vein, the committee considered recommending a centralized structure that would provide tools for building ontologies, practice principles, training, and other resources. However, in addition to the likely prohibitive scope and cost of such a structure, we recognized that, while some in the field might welcome the clarity it could bring, others would surely reject such a top-down governance model. It is not clear how such an entity would function in a world of ontological pluralism and how such a centralized entity would manage to reconcile differences in understanding of concepts, classifications, and other complex issues in all of the behavioral science disciplines.

At the other end of the spectrum of possibilities, one could simply hope that ontologies will develop organically. The committee believes this would be unwise: that approach has yielded the current situation. Therefore, we have chosen a middle position by focusing on ways to expand available resources and incentives, to stimulate grassroots ontology development, and to coordinate efforts, with the aim of pushing for ontologies to be a higher priority in behavioral science research.

Agencies of the federal government are best positioned to provide the coordination and resources needed for this kind of activity, so we direct two broad recommendations to NIH and other agencies. Ontology development often does not fit within categories commonly supported by research awards. At NIH, the Division of Program Coordination, Planning, and Strategic Initiatives (DPCPSI) oversees cross-institute initiatives and includes offices for behavioral and social science research, prevention research, women's health, AIDS research, tribal health, diet and nutrition research, and research infrastructure. It also includes programs that use ontologies, such as those on data science and portfolio analysis. Because of its vast reach within NIH, DPCPSI is in a unique position to demonstrate how ontologies can improve the way behavioral science knowledge is created, understood, and used.

RECOMMENDATION 1: The National Institutes of Health (NIH) and the National Science Foundation (NSF) should develop formal agendas for accelerating behavioral science research through the development and use of semantically formal ontologies. These agendas should draw on ideas generated within other scientific domains and the international scientific community and should include a range of activities:

- NIH should use its convening authority to engage experts and to develop a plan for ontology development across NIH institutes and centers. The plan should illustrate how NIH resources might be used to develop ontologies; link them to existing ontologies; and apply them in the interest of higher quality, more replicable behavioral research and improved behavioral health, including through criteria for funding research efforts.
- Within NIH, the Behavioral and Social Science Coordinating Committee should propose a plan for ontology development across NIH institutes and centers.
- The NIH Division of Program Coordination, Planning, and Strategic Initiatives should develop an ontology for classifying intramural and extramural behavioral research at NIH.
- The NSF Social, Behavioral and Economic Science Directorate should coordinate ontology development efforts with the NSF Computer, Information Science, and Engineering Directorate.
- NIH and NSF should collaborate in providing transition grants to allow ontology centers to develop business plans and distribution models that could put them on a sustainable footing.

- The National Library of Medicine should bolster the training it offers in biomedical informatics to strengthen the capacity of the people who will lead the development of the next generation of scientific ontologies.
- To avoid duplication and overlap, NIH and NSF ontology development efforts should be coordinated through the NIH Office of Behavioral and Social Sciences Research and the NSF Social, Behavioral and Economic Sciences Directorate.

RECOMMENDATION 2: The National Institutes of Health, the National Science Foundation, and other agencies that support research should seek and encourage opportunities to fund work that will support continuing progress in the development and use of ontologies in the behavioral sciences, such as research on technological supports for ontology development, the ways scientists develop and use ontologies across diverse fields, and institutional supports and structures that support ontology use in diverse fields.

RECOMMENDATION 3: The Office of Science and Technology Policy should develop a report on how an explicit formal specification of a shared conceptualization for behavioral science can be implemented across federal science agencies, based on review of ontologies developed by other agencies including, but not limited to, the National Science Foundation; the Departments of Health and Human Services, Defense, Transportation, Agriculture, Labor, and Justice; the Environmental Protection Agency; the National Institute of Standards and Technology; the National Oceanic and Atmospheric Administration; and the Defense Advanced Research Projects Agency.

Professional organizations and publishers also have a key role to play, and we direct recommendations to such organizations. The Federation of Associations in Behavioral and Brain Sciences (FABBS) and the Consortium of Social Science Associations (COSSA) represent most professional and scientific organizations in the behavioral and social sciences. FABBS promotes advancing the sciences of mind, brain, and behavior, and its mission includes training and fostering communication among scientists. The COSSA membership includes professional associations, scientific societies, research centers and institutes, colleges and universities, and industry affiliates.

Similarly, there are two major academic publishers in the behavioral sciences. The American Psychological Association is the largest publisher of behavioral science journals, and the Association for Psychological Science is also a leader in scientific publication. In addition, both organizations work with the Council of Graduate Departments of Psychology to coordinate and provide accreditation for educational programs and in psychology. We call out these organizations because they have wide reach, but we hope that similar organizations will also take part in the community building necessary to develop and encourage understanding of what ontologies can offer in the behavioral sciences.

RECOMMENDATION 4: The Federation of Associations in Behavioral and Brain Sciences and the Consortium of Social Science Associations, along with similar organizations, should coordinate ontology development across academic and professional organizations.

RECOMMENDATION 5: The American Psychological Association Council of Editors and the Association for Psychological Science editorial office, along with similar organizations, should develop policies to improve the use of common vocabularies and data-reporting standards in behavioral science journals.

RECOMMENDATION 6: The Council of Graduate Departments of Psychology, the Education Directorate of the American Psychological Association, and the Education Office of the Association for Psychological Science, along with similar organizations, should create strategies to integrate ontology development into graduate-level teaching and practical training.

The goals of our recommendations are to strengthen approaches to categorizing and defining the concepts and phenomena behavioral scientists study and to develop ways to better leverage contemporary technologies in structuring knowledge about human behavior. These ideas build on what has been accomplished through centuries of attempts to synthesize what is known, as well as decades of research on human and animal behavior. The approaches we recommend have the potential to democratize knowledge about human behavior by making that knowledge efficiently retrievable and actionable by the wide diversity of stakeholders in the domain of the behavioral sciences. Ultimately, better communications within the scientific community and between scientists and knowledge consumers will improve the science of behavior, the way it is disseminated, and its capacity to ameliorate and prevent suffering. This report is focused on the behavioral sciences, but most of the issues discussed here would also apply in other domains, and the committee hopes they will be of use in the overall advancement of science.

REFERENCES

Cella, D., and Hays, R. (2021). *Ontological Issues in Patient Reported Outcomes: Conceptual Issues and Challenges Addressed by the Patient-Reported Outcomes Measurement Information System (PROMIS®)*. Commissioned paper prepared for the Committee on Accelerating Behavioral Science through Ontology Development and Use, National Academies of Sciences, Engineering, and Medicine. Available: https://nap.nationalacademies.org/resource/26464/Cella-and-Hays-comissioned-paper.pdf

Larsen, K.R., Michie, S., Hekler, E.B., Gibson, B., Spruijt-Metz, D., Ahern, D., Cole-Lewis, H., Ellis, R.J., Hesse, B., Moser, R.P., and Yi, J. (2017). Behavior change interventions: The potential of ontologies for advancing science and practice. *Journal of Behavioral Medicine, 40*(1), 6–22. https://doi.org/10.1007/s10865-016-9768-0

Appendix A

Ontological Systems Referenced in the Report

Ontology	Brief Description	Links
Cognitive Atlas	A collaborative effort to describe how the human brain processes information, involving investigators with expertise in psychology, biology, neuroscience, neurology, linguistics, and other disciplines.	https://www.cognitiveatlas.org/
PROMIS®	A measurement tool for harmonizing measures of patient outcomes.	https://commonfund.nih.gov/promis/index
NCI Thesaurus	A regularly updated resource of definitions of biomedical terms and relationships among them that was designed to make it easier for researchers to share data.	https://ncithesaurus.nci.nih.gov/ncitbrowser/
BioPortal	A central website for locating biomedical ontologies.	https://bioportal.bioontology.org/
Big Five Personality Traits	A suggested grouping of personality traits. The grouping provides a model of the primary dimensions of individual differences in personality.	https://dictionary.apa.org/big-five-personality-model
Thesaurus of Psychological Index Terms	A controlled list of standardized terms and definitions of psychological concepts with a loose hierarchy showing relationships to other terms. The controlled vocabulary allows for indexing, cataloging, and searching of psychological concepts.	https://www.apa.org/pubs/databases/training/thesaurus

Ontology	Brief Description	Links
The Hierarchical Taxonomy of Psychopathology (HiTOP)	A dimensional classification system of a wide range of psychiatric problems. Hierarchical relationships in HiTOP allow for improved classification of psychopathology dimensions to facilitate research and clinical practice.	https://hitop.unt.edu/introduction
Research Domain Criteria (RDoC)	A taxonomy of psychopathology that integrates many levels of information from genomics to behavioral processes. RDoC provides a framework to understand the nature of mental health and illness in terms of varying degrees of dysfunction in general psychological/biological systems.	https://www.nimh.nih.gov/research/research-funded-by-nimh/rdoc
Diagnostic and Statistical Manual of Mental Disorders (DSM)	A classification of mental disorders using a common language and standard criteria. The DSM features descriptions of mental health conditions based on categories and is used as a diagnostic tool.	https://www.psychiatry.org/psychiatrists/practice/dsm
International Classification of Diseases (ICD)	A categorization system for physical and mental illnesses. The ICD classifies signs and symptoms, abnormal findings, complaints, social circumstances, and external causes of illness or diseases.	https://www.who.int/standards/classifications/classification-of-diseases
Behavioral Change Intervention Ontology (BCIO)	An ontology with a defined set of entities and their relationships using a common language. BCIO is used to organize information in a form that enables efficient accumulation of knowledge and enables links to other knowledge systems.	https://www.ebi.ac.uk/ols/ontologies/bcio
Gene Ontology	The Gene Ontology provides human-readable and machine-readable information on the functions of genes and has been designed to serve as a foundation for computational analysis of large-scale molecular biology and genetics experiments in biomedical research.	http://geneontology.org/

Appendix B

Example Use Cases Generated in a Committee Self-Survey

Actor	Context	Expected Goal	Resource	Stakeholder
A therapist planning treatment	in a mental health clinic	to improve clinical outcomes	using a tool that summarizes all treatments	patients
A student reviewing literature	in graduate school	to prepare a dissertation	using an ontology of brain injury	self
A parent investigating a child's problem	at home	to determine whether the problem is serious	using an ontology of symptoms	parent and child
A policy maker exploring engagement strategies	during a pandemic	to promote use of masking and social distancing	using an ontology of engagement practices	the general public
An elementary school teacher who wants to engage her students	in their classroom	to improve social behavior	using an ontology of social skills	their students
A pediatrician reviewing research	in a doctor's office	to offer guidance on better sleep	using a search tool on sleep problems	patients
A medical clinician	in a clinical setting	to provide a diagnosis and treatment plan	using an ontology of symptoms and disorders	other clinicians and patients
Clinical researchers	in clinical and research settings	to develop and test behavioral interventions	using an ontology of constructs related to emotional well-being	other clinical researchers, clinicians, and policy makers
A cognitive neuroscientist interested in social cognition	in a research setting	to understand the nomological net to understand and organize social cognition	using an ontology of social systems and processes	other neuroscientists and clinical researchers interested in social cognition and mechanism underlying psychopathology
A graduate student in clinical psychology	in a clinical or educational setting	to improve knowledge about psychopathology and learn how to diagnose effectively	using an ontology of signs and symptoms of psychopathology	other clinical students and professors

A program officer at the National Institutes of Health (NIH)	in clinical and research settings	to write requests for proposals that can stimulate the development of brain-informed treatment protocols	using an ontology of brain correlates associated with signs and symptoms of psychopathology	NIH clinical researchers
A professor of the philosophy of the human mind	in a research setting	to derive conclusions about consciousness informed by empirical science	using an ontology of validated cognitive constructs	other professors, cognitive neuroscientists, and clinical researchers
An officer responsible for helping new immigrants acclimate to a new country	in any setting	to develop a digestible synthesis of available resources that make the process of integrating in a new state or country understandable	through access to Web pages of government or state resources	immigrants
Law enforcement officers and lawmakers explaining the rights and responsibilities of individuals in a specific situation at hand (e.g., for voting)	in any setting	to empower citizens to take ownership of the process	with documents detailing the relevant laws	citizens, the general public
Financial advisors	in any setting	to educate people about how to best manage money and finances	with documents that codify best practices for managing credit and other aspects of finances	the general public, particularly people from disadvantaged backgrounds
A researcher studying a new field	formal or informal education	to develop a synthesis of the documents that gives the researcher a big-picture view of the field and facilitates learning	using sets of documents (books, scientific articles, etc.) chosen by researchers	self

continued

Actor	Context	Expected Goal	Resource	Stakeholder
A person learning a new language (e.g., English)	in any setting	to facilitate learning through the organization of key concepts and their relationships in both languages, as well as correspondence between the two	with a dictionary translating to/from person's mother tongue from/to English	self
Mental health counselors	in a clinic or similar setting	to improve patient care with the organization of notes on the patient's habits/behaviors, how they relate to each other, and how they affect the patient between visits to counselors	with notes taken by the patient or caretakers to monitor behavior and the effect of treatments on a day-to-day basis when away from counselor	patients
A behavioral scientist	in a research lab, classroom	Move the field toward greater use of common manipulations, definitions, instruments, constructs, etc.	with a shared set of construct names, definitions, and operationalizations in a specific behavioral science domain (e.g., emotion regulation)	graduate students and fellow researchers
Mental health clinicians	in clinical or similar setting	to develop clearer links from models of psychopathology to a priori selected interventions based on established mechanisms of action	with a functional taxonomy of emotion regulation dysfunctions	patients

The NIH director	in research and administrative settings	to encourage standardization and sharing across research groups and enhance knowledge integration	using reliable and valid classification of topics for behavioral intervention research	funding agencies, Congress, the general public
Research foundations	in research and clinical settings	to enhance standardization and sharing across research groups for the increased likelihood of cumulative and synergistic knowledge increase	using a systematic taxonomy of research topics relevant to the foundation's mission (e.g., anxiety and depressive disorders)	foundation beneficiaries and the public
Social scientists	in academia and applied research settings	to identify existing synergies and inconsistencies and encourage cross-disciplinary exploration	using a taxonomy for an overarching construct/ domain of knowledge, such as emotion	the social science disciplines broadly construed, both quantitative and interpretive
Medical and other children's experts	at home and in doctors' offices	to improve communication among experts, patients, and families, to improve children's mental health	using an ontology of key symptoms and disorders that arise during a pandemic like COVID	parents and their children
Health providers	in a waiting room in a hospital or clinic	to improve their knowledge of vaccine and encourage vaccination	using an ontology as a knowledge base for vaccine education and promotion	patients and their guardians
Biomedical informaticians	online	to infer possible new hypotheses	using an ontology as a knowledge graph that semantically integrates biomedical knowledge extracted from different sources	scientists

continued

Actor	Context	Expected Goal	Resource	Stakeholder
Public health researchers	in any setting	to gather information about people's health beliefs to provide needed interventions	using an ontology as an information model to formally describe health belief models	the general public
Nutrition experts	with a mobile app	to help users to manage their diets	using an ontology to model related facts for fast and other food	the general public
Public health researchers	in any setting	to ensure semantic interoperability	using an ontology to formally model social determinants of health	public health researchers
Information curator	online	to help them navigate the complex world of health information in an organized way	using ontology-structured knowledge of a disease, treatment, outcomes	patients, caregivers, and clinicians
Researchers	in publications and research studies	to improve the reusability of an existing dataset and the reproducibility of study results	using annotated datasets with measurements	other researchers
Funding agencies	online	to identify key areas where additional research are needed, to bridge the gaps in people's mental models	using standardized terminology and data resources to guide funding investments and harmonize study results across projects	researchers
Researchers, funding agencies, and data producer	online	to produce harmonized datasets that have clear semantic definitions of variables, study designs, and other features	using ontology-based metadata to support semantic integration of different data resources	researchers

Researchers	online	to standardize and communicate the important blocks of studies to ensure reproducibility	using annotated study designs and executable documentation of studies, such as an ontology-annotated reporting of a study	other researchers
Member of the general public	online	to gain insight into possible explanations of symptoms	using an ontology of symptoms and disorders	self or family member
Biomedical informatics researchers	doing system development in a lab	for more effective use of ontology in clinical applications	using technical details of ontology construction and access	users of results in applications
A health care provider	in a clinical practice	to enhance decision making	with an ontology for underlying clinical decision support	providers and their patients
A graduate school instructor on patient safety	in a classroom	to link medical errors to various cognitive factors	using a taxonomy and an ontology of medical errors	graduate students
Public health worker	in a community	to enhance public health interventions	using an ontology of public health linking various health-related factors under consideration	the general public and policy makers
A behavioral intervention scientist	in clinical trials of behavior change	to understand and change behavior	using an ontology of behavior change components	health care providers
A behavior science theorist	in research, literature reviews, and theory proposals	to advance theory	using an ontology of theories of behavior change	graduate students

continued

Actor	Context	Expected Goal	Resource	Stakeholder
Policy makers	in health departments	to investigate epidemiological advances in describing the health of the public	using an ontology of human health behavior	the general public
A behavioral scientist mentor	in a social behavioral research team	to improve the rigor of proposed studies	using an ontology of behavioral measures	junior scientists
A professor who is teaching	in an applied research methods course	to improve knowledge of social/behavioral research	using an ontology of behavioral measures	graduate students
An expert panel that has been asked for advice	for future funding announcements	to inform priority research areas	using an ontology of behavioral measures	funding agencies
A researcher on health disparities collaborating with other researchers	for an NIH grant proposal	to identify risk and protective factors of health disparities	using an ontology for cultural/ethnic measures of behavior	health care providers

Appendix C

Biographical Sketches of Committee on Accelerating Behavioral Science through Ontology Development and Use

CHAIR

Robert M. Kaplan (NAM) is a faculty member at the Stanford School of Medicine Clinical Excellence Research Center. He previously served as chief science officer at the U.S. Agency for Healthcare Research and Quality (AHRQ) and as associate director of the National Institutes of Health, where he led the behavioral and social sciences programs. He is also a distinguished research professor of health policy and management at the University of California, Los Angeles (UCLA), where he previously led the UCLA/RAND AHRQ health services training program and the UCLA/RAND Centers for Disease Control Prevention Research Center. He was formerly chair of the Department of Health Services and professor and chair of the Department of Family and Preventive Medicine, at the University of California, San Diego. He is a past president of five different national or international professional organizations and has served as editor-in-chief for two academic journals. He has a Ph.D. in psychology from the University of California, Riverside.

COMMITTEE

Demba Ba serves as associate professor of electrical engineering and bioengineering in Harvard University's School of Engineering and Applied Sciences, where he directs the Chesapeake Regional Information System for our Patients group. Recently, he has taken a keen interest in the connection between artificial neural networks and sparse signal processing. His group leverages this connection to solve data-driven unsupervised learning problems in neuroscience, to understand the principles of hierarchical representations of sensory signals in the brain, and to develop explainable artificial intelligence. Previously, he was a postdoctoral associate with the MIT/Harvard Neuroscience Statistics Research Laboratory, where he developed theory and efficient algorithms to assess synchrony among large assemblies of neurons. He has a Ph.D. in electrical engineering and computer science with a minor in mathematics from the Massachusetts Institute of Technology. In 2021, Harvard's Faculty of Arts and Sciences awarded him the Roslyn Abramson award for outstanding undergraduate teaching.

Lisa Feldman Barrett is a university distinguished professor at Northeastern University with appointments at the Massachusetts General Hospital (MGH) and Harvard Medical School. Her lab is developing a systems-level model of brain and body mechanisms to unify human affect, emotion, motivation, cognition, and action. She is the recipient of a National Institutes of Health Director's Pioneer Award for transformative research, Guggenheim Fellowship in neuroscience, the Mentor Award for Lifetime Achievement from the Association for Psychological Science, and the Distinguished Scientific Contribution Award from the American Psychological Association. She is an elected fellow of the American Academy of Arts and Sciences, the Royal Society of Canada, and a number of other honorific societies. She is also a former president of the APS. She is the Chief Science Officer for the Center for Law, Brain and Behavior at MGH, and actively engages in informal science education. She has a Ph.D. in clinical psychology from the University of Waterloo.

Jiang Bian is the associate director of the Biomedical Informatics program for the Clinical and Translational Sciences Institute at the University of Florida and the director of the Cancer Informatics Shared Resource for the University of Florida Health Cancer Center, where he is also an associate professor in biomedical informatics. His background is in data sciences, working with heterogeneous data, information, and knowledge resources. His research focuses on data-driven medicine with applications of informatics techniques, including artificial intelligence and machine learning methods in medicine in order to solve big and heterogeneous data problems. He is focused on data mining, including the social Web, to provide insights into health-related behavior and health outcomes of various populations for development of interventions that promote public and consumer health. He is also focused on development of novel informatics methods, specifically systems to support clinical and clinical research activities, such as tools for semantic data integration, data-driven clinical trial design, and cohort discovery. He has a Ph.D. in integrated computing from the University of Arkansas at Little Rock.

Katy Börner is the Victor H. Yngve distinguished professor of engineering and information science in the Departments of Intelligent Systems Engineering and Information Science at the Luddy School of Informatics, Computing, and Engineering. She is core faculty of the cognitive science program and the founding director of the Cyberinfrastructure for Network Science Center at Indiana University. She is a fellow of the American Association for the Advancement of Science, a Humboldt Research fellow, and an Association for Computing Machinery fellow. She also serves as a curator of the international Places & Spaces: Mapping Science exhibit. Her research focuses on the development of data analysis and visualization techniques for information access, understanding, and management. She is particularly interested in the formalization, measurement, and systematic improvement of people's data visualization literacy; the study of the structure and evolution of scientific disciplines; the analysis and visualization of online activity; and the development of cyberinfrastructures for large-scale scientific collaboration and computation. She has a Ph.D. from the University of Kaiserslautern.

Bruce F. Chorpita is a professor of psychology and professor of psychiatry and biobehavioral sciences at the University of California, Los Angeles. He was the lead developer for the intensive component of PRIDE, a project designed to develop, test, and disseminate effective treatments and training model for lay counselors to address anxiety, depression, and anger problems in adolescents in India. He is the principal investigator for the Reaching Families multisite trial and the lead author of the MATCH-ADTC protocol. Previously, he held a faculty position with the department of psychology at the University of Hawaii, and he served as the clinical director of the Hawaii Department of Health's Child and Adolescent Mental Health Division. His ongoing research is aimed at improving the effectiveness of mental health service systems for children through innovation in mental health treatment design, clinical decision making, information-delivery models, and service system architecture. He received his Ph.D. in psychology from the University at Albany, State University of New York.

David Danks* is professor of data science and philosophy and affiliate faculty in computer science and engineering at the University of California, San Diego. His research interests are at the intersection of philosophy, cognitive science, and machine learning, using ideas, methods, and frameworks from each to advance our understanding of complex, interdisciplinary problems. He has examined the ethical, psychological, and policy issues around AI

---

* Committee Member as of July 29, 2021.

and robotics in transportation, health care, privacy, and security. He has also done research in computational cognitive science, culminating in his *Unifying the Mind: Cognitive Representations as Graphical Models*, and he has developed multiple novel causal discovery algorithms for complex types of observational and experimental data. He is the recipient of a James S. McDonnell Foundation Scholar Award, as well as an Andrew Carnegie Fellowship. He was previously L.L. Thurstone professor of philosophy and psychology and head of the department of philosophy at Carnegie Mellon University (CMU). He also served as the chief ethicist of CMU's Block Center for Technology & Society; co-director of CMU's Center for Informed Democracy and Social Cybersecurity; and an adjunct member of the Heinz College of Information Systems and Public Policy and the CMU's Neuroscience Institute. He received an A.B. in philosophy from Princeton University and a Ph.D. in philosophy from the University of California, San Diego.

Karina W. Davidson is dean of academic affairs, director of the Institute of Health System Science at the Feinstein Institutes for Medical Research, Endowed Donald and Barbara Zucker professor in health outcomes at the Zucker School of Medicine, and senior vice president, research at Northwell Health. For more than 25 years she has served in leadership roles for teams focused on the advancement of scientific and patient care missions. Her current research focuses on personalized (N-of-1) trials to identify precision therapies to improve a single patient's symptoms, conditions, or behaviors, and promote their overall health and wellness. Many of her National Institutes of Health-funded randomized controlled trials additionally focus on changing both clinician and patient behavior, to ultimately improve length or quality of patient life. She has a Ph.D. in clinical health psychology and an M.A.Sc in industrial/organizational psychology. Davidson currently serves as chair of the United States Preventive Services Task Force.

Randall Engle (NAS)** is a professor at Georgia Institute of Technology. His research focuses on cognition and brain science. His interests include working memory capacity and its relationship to the concept of attention control. He is a member of the National Academy of Sciences, American Psychological Association (fellow), American Psychological Society (fellow), the Society of Experimental Psychologists, the Psychonomic Society, Memory Disorders Research Society, Sigma Xi, and The Scientific Research Society. He has a Ph.D. in experimental psychology from The Ohio State University.

** Committee Member until May 19, 2021.

Catherine A. Hartley is an associate professor of psychology and neural science at New York University (NYU). She is co-director of the NYU Institute for the Study of Decision Making and co-director of the NYU Max Planck Center for Language Music and Emotion. Her research aims to characterize changes in cognitive representations and computations that inform learning and decision making across development, and the neural dynamics that give rise to these changes. In this work, she leverages diverse methodological approaches including neuroimaging, computational modeling, and psychophysiology. A central goal of her research is to understand how specific learning and decision making biases contribute to vulnerability or resilience to psychopathology. She is an Association for Psychological Science (APS) fellow and a recipient of the National Institute of Mental Health Biobehavioral Research Award for Innovative New Scientists, the National Science Foundation CAREER Award, and APS Janet Taylor Spence Award for Transformative Early Career Contributions. She has a Ph.D. in experimental psychology from NYU.

Mark A. Musen (NAM) is a professor of biomedical informatics at Stanford University, where he is the director of the Stanford Center for Biomedical Informatics Research. He conducts research related to open science, data stewardship, intelligent systems, and biomedical decision support. His group developed Protégé, the world's most widely used technology for building and managing terminologies and ontologies. He has served as principal investigator of the National Center for Biomedical Ontology and the Center for Expanded Data Annotation and Retrieval. He chaired the Health Informatics and Modeling Topic Advisory Group for the World Health Organization (WHO)'s revision of the International Classification of Diseases and he currently directs the WHO Collaborating Center for Classification, Terminology, and Standards at Stanford University. He has been elected to the American College of Medical Informatics, the Association of American Physicians, the International Academy of Health Sciences Informatics, and the National Academy of Medicine. He is founding co-editor-in-chief of the journal *Applied Ontology*. He received his M.D. from Brown University and his Ph.D. in medical information sciences from Stanford University.

Vimla L. Patel is a senior research scientist and director of the Center for Cognitive Studies in Medicine and Public Health at the New York Academy of Medicine. Previously, she was a professor of medicine and the director of Cognitive Science Center at McGill University. Her early research focused on scientific foundations for medical and health education, particularly in cognitive foundations of medical decision making. She is an elected fellow of the Royal Society of Canada (Academy of Social Sciences), the American

College of Medical Informatics, and the New York Academy of Medicine, and she is a recipient of the Swedish Woman of Science award. She is an associate editor of the *Journal of Biomedical Informatics* and sits on the editorial boards of *Intelligence-based Medicine* and *Advances in Health Science Education*. She has a Ph.D. in educational and cognitive psychology from McGill University.

Frank Puga is an assistant professor in the department of acute, chronic and continuing care at the University of Alabama at Birmingham School of Nursing. His expertise includes stress, resilience, and mental health in older adults living with chronic illness. His research focuses on inter- and intra-individual variation in mental health experiences over time and factors that increase resilience to stress in older adults, specifically among diverse patient populations disproportionately impacted by dementia and cancer. The main goal of his work is to develop and test cognitive and behavioral interventions that promote healthy aging. He received his Ph.D. in psychology with a concentration in behavioral neuroscience from the University of Texas at Austin.

Carla Sharp is a professor of psychology and associate dean for faculty and research at the University of Houston (UH). She also directs the Developmental Psychopathology Lab at UH. Her main research focus is on social cognition as it relates to disorders of attachment disruption in children and adolescents, with a special interest in borderline personality disorder. Her books include *Social Cognition and Developmental Psychopathology* and the *Handbook of Borderline Personality Disorder in Children and Adolescents*. She is currently interested in the metastructure of psychopathology to determine the cross-cutting value of social cognition in alternative models of personality pathology and as target of treatment. She received her Ph.D. in clinical psychology from the University of Cambridge.

Timothy J. Strauman is a professor and former chair of the department of psychology and neuroscience at Duke University and also professor of psychiatry and behavioral sciences in the Duke University School of Medicine. His research interests focus on the psychological and neurobiological processes of self-regulation, conceptualized in terms of a cognitive/motivational perspective, as well as on the relation between self-regulation and affect and how such processes might contribute to psychopathology. His lab's clinically focused research includes the development and validation of a new self-regulation-based therapy for depression, self-system therapy, and the use of neuroimaging techniques to examine the mechanisms of action of treatments for depression. He is a former president of the Academy of Psychological Clinical Science, a fellow of the Association for Psychological

Science, a current member of the Board on Behavioral, Cognitive, and Sensory Sciences, and a founding fellow of the Academy of Cognitive Therapy. He has a Ph.D. in psychology from New York University.

Cui Tao is the Doris L. Ross professor of biomedical informatics and director of the Center for Biomedical Semantics and Data Intelligence at The University of Texas Health Science Center at Houston. Her background is in clinical informatics and computer science, and her research interests include ontologies, standard terminologies, semantic Web, information extraction and integration, machine learning, as well as applying these technologies to clinical and translational studies. She is a recipient of the Presidential Early Career Awards for Scientists and Engineers, the highest honor bestowed by the U.S. government on science and engineering professionals in the early stages of their independent research careers. She has a Ph.D. in computer science from Brigham Young University.

James F. Woodward is a distinguished professor in the department of history and philosophy of science at the University of Pittsburgh. Previously, he was the J.O. and Juliette Koepfli professor of humanities at the California Institute of Technology. He is a fellow of the American Academy of Arts and Sciences, a fellow of the American Association for the Advancement of Science, and former president of the Philosophy of Science Association. His research covers a number of different areas, including theories of causation, explanation and inductive inference in general philosophy of science, philosophy of psychology, and philosophy of social science. His interests in psychology include the empirical psychology of causal learning and judgment. He also maintains an interest in moral psychology and the empirical study of human behavior in morally significant situations.